GENTLING
the
HEART

GENTLING
the
HEART

Buddhist Loving-Kindness Practice for Christians

Mary Jo Meadow

CROSSROAD · NEW YORK

1994

The Crossroad Publishing Company
370 Lexington Avenue, New York, NY 10017

Copyright © 1994 by Mary Jo Meadow

Printed in the United States of America

Library of Congress Cataloging-in-Publication Data

Meadow, Mary Jo, 1936–
    Gentling the heart : Buddhist loving-kindness practice for
Christians / Mary Jo Meadow.
      p. cm.
    Includes bibliographical references.
    ISBN 0-8245-1434-3
    1. Compassion (Buddhism) 2. Love—Religious aspects—Buddhism.
3. Love—Religious aspects—Christianity. 4. Christian life.
5. Religious life—Buddhism. 6. Buddhism—Doctrines. I. Title.
BQ4360.M43   1994
294.3'5699—dc20   94-25821
                                                      CIP

*For Joseph Goldstein,
with deep respect, love,
and gratitude*

Love your neighbor as yourself.

—Jesus, the Christ

*One who loves oneself
can never harm another.*

—Gotama, the Buddha

CONTENTS

PREFACE

D O YOU WANT to develop a loving heart toward other beings? Since you picked up this book, you probably do. You have realized that this is an important part of spiritual life and practice. When Jesus was asked what the most important commandment was, he said that the first is: " 'Love the Lord your God with all your heart and with all your soul and with all your mind and with all your strength.' The second is this: 'Love your neighbor as yourself.' There is no commandment greater than these" (Mark 12:30–31). Love God with your whole being, and love your neighbor as yourself. These two great commandments contain all that God asks of us. Some have called them the vertical and the horizontal directions in spiritual practice.

This book teaches you a Buddhist meditation practice that cultivates an attitude of gentle, universal, impartial loving-kindness toward all. It helps you grow in the horizontal direction of spiritual practice. It can bring you to the proper love of self that makes possible the proper love of others. This tradition does not believe that we should always submerge our own interests for the sake of others or choose to put ourselves last. Buddhists teach that our love is not genuine if it does not care equally for ourselves, and that proper self-love brings with it proper love for others.

We should exclude no one and prefer no one. We make everyone our kin. "Someone told Jesus, 'Your mother and brothers are standing outside, wanting to speak to you.' He replied, 'Who is my mother, and who are my brothers?' Pointing to his disciples, he said, 'Here are my mother and my brothers' " (Matt. 12:47–50). We become able to say this of all beings.

FOR THE READER

This book was written primarily for Christians who want to learn a practical method of meditation to help them follow the teachings of Jesus about love. However, anyone who wants the heart-deliverance of loving-kindness will find help here.

Our primary sources are both Christian and Buddhist scriptures. We also draw from the Christian Carmelite saints, mystics, and doctors of the church Teresa of Avila and John of the Cross to illustrate some points about meditation and spiritual practice.[1] Two other major Buddhist sources are the *Visuddhimagga* (*The Path of Purification*), a fifth-century Buddhist classic on meditation practice, and the writing of the great Burmese meditation master Mahasi Sayadaw on loving-kindness practice.[2]

THE WORD "LOVE"

"Love" is a difficult word in the English language. Where many other languages have different words to describe different kinds of love experience, English has only one word. Affectionate love within families, love we have for friends with shared values and interests, playful love for people we just have fun with, the passion of erotic love, calm and uneventful love for people who have quietly grown into a connection with our lives, love for our own being, universal love for all beings, and love for God — all are often simply called "love."

While all these can truly be love, many experiences that do not properly fit the word are also called "love." Some people consider either sentimentality or lust to be love. Others think love necessarily implies jealousy and possessiveness. Some think love must always be doing something or fixing something. For others, love can exist only when there is frequent contact between lover and loved one. What is called love is often a conditional relationship; our love depends upon the other party's behaving or being a certain way.

IMPARTIAL, UNIVERSAL LOVE

Christians have used the Greek word *agape* to describe a state of universal, impartial caring and good will toward all people, loving them simply because they are. This Jesus told us to do. "A new command I give you: Love one another. As I have loved you, so you must love one another" (John 13:34).

The Buddhist scriptures have a similar word, *metta* (pronounced "met'tah"), from the Pali language of the Buddha. It comes from a root stem that means gentle friendliness. Another derivation from that stem refers to being a friend in need. *Metta* is usually translated "loving-kindness," the best English word to capture the flavor of its meaning. It is very much like the stance defined by the beatitude "Blessed are the gentle, for they will inherit the earth" (Matt. 5:5). The Dalai Lama, spiritual head of Tibetan Buddhism, has said many times, "My religion is kindness."

Metta, this attitude of universal loving-kindness or gentle friendliness, has immediately obvious similarities to Christian *agape;* however, we will point them out in even more detail for you. One conclusion becomes very clear: that all the great spiritualities recognize the need for a universally loving heart. On this we will be judged. "I tell you the truth, whatever you did for one of the least of these brothers or sisters of mine, you did for me.... Whatever you did not do for one of the least of these, you did not do for me" (Matt. 25:40, 45).

TWO FORMS OF
BUDDHIST MEDITATION PRACTICE

In *Purifying the Heart: Buddhist Insight Meditation for Christians*, with my colleagues Fathers Kevin Culligan and Daniel Chowning, I give you one time-honored practice from Theravadan Buddhism.[3] Insight meditation strongly fosters the vertical dimension of spirituality, loving God with all our being. This practice bares us to ourselves, bringing the self-knowledge that St. John of the Cross said is essential. It encourages renunciation and aspiration to know God, fostering the radical self-emptying that makes possible the inflow of God into the soul. It puts us into the beatitude "Blessed are the pure in heart, for they will see God" (Matt. 5:8). In exposing to us our own suffering, it also indirectly helps develop compassion and caring toward others.

Theravadan Buddhism has another equally honored practice, that of *metta,* or loving-kindness. Its thrust is directly toward the horizontal dimension in spiritual practice. It aims to transform the human heart into love and is ruthless when it finds anything less than pure love in the heart. Gradually it exposes and heals the envies, resentments, hatreds, jealousies, annoyances, and impatience that distance us from others. We become able to do as Jesus told us: "But I tell you who hear me: Love your enemies, do good to those who hate you, bless those who curse you, pray for those who mistreat you" (Luke 6:27–28).

Purifying the Heart gives you just enough information to do informal *metta* practice as an adjunct to insight practice, which is the focus of that book. In this book, *metta* is taught in its own right, and the full classical practice is given. It is not necessary to have done insight practice to learn *metta* practice. This book and *Purifying the Heart* are both written in the same spirit; both offer a practice from the Buddhist tradition helpful for strengthening Christian spiritual life according to the directives of Vatican II.[4]

In traditional Buddhist monastic practice, the monk or

nun often started meditation work with *metta,* loving-kindness practice. This develops concentration at the same time that it builds gentle friendliness toward all. The concentration and healing of the heart that it promotes provided a good monastic start. Only after becoming quite proficient in this practice would they begin insight practice.

In more recent times, many people — especially lay people — begin with insight practice. At some point, the value of adding loving-kindness meditation is seen, and it also becomes part of a person's spiritual practice. Whichever you learn first, these two forms of meditation together make a complete practice.

PLAN OF THE BOOK

This book emphasizes practice, although you are also given enough background information to understand loving-kindness. The book's first part gives historical and other background information about *metta,* including traditional suggestions for preparing for *metta* practice.

In Part II, we teach you the classical Theravadan Buddhist form for practicing *metta.* You also learn how to develop the three other *brahmaviharas* (bruh'muh-vee-hah'ruhs), or "heavenly attitudes," that are typically cultivated along with *metta.* These are compassion, delight in the happiness of others, and equanimity. Part III offers some contemporary variations with which you might work once you are proficient in *brahmavihara* practice.

Part IV is the most technical, describing types of meditation. It explains common problems in doing concentrative meditation and suggests some remedies for them. This part also outlines stages in the development of deepening concentration that occurs with practice.

An appendix gives you some variant phrases for practice, and another includes Pali language forms. Other appendices present both a traditional chant and others, set in a simple plain chant form, for either personal or para-liturgical use.

ACKNOWLEDGMENTS

This book rests upon the helpfulness of many people. A very special thanks goes to Joseph Goldstein, Buddhist author and co-founder and guiding teacher at Insight Meditation Society in Barre, Massachusetts.[5] As my principal Buddhist teacher from the start of my practice, he has freely given me time, energy, and deep understanding as he guided both my insight and *brahmavihara* practices. His influence pervades this book. Its dedication to him is one small way I try to express the deep respect, love, and gratitude I feel for him.

The Venerable Sayadaw U Pandita, Anagarika Sri Munindra, and Sharon Salzberg have also given me considerable help and support in practice. I thank them, too, and also the other Buddhist teachers under whose guidance I have practiced: Venerable U Pannathami, Venerable U Pannadipa, Venerable U Dammika, and Steven Armstrong.

I thank my colleagues in leading the "Silence and Awareness" retreats, Kevin Culligan, OCD, and Daniel Chowning, OCD, for continuing friendship and support in spiritual life. Resources for Ecumenical Spirituality, sponsor of our retreats, provided space and atmosphere for writing in its forest monastery.[6]

I am indebted to Andrew Olendzki of Insight Meditation Society for help with Pali language phrases. IMS teacher Steven Smith helped me locate scriptural passages. Steven Armstrong provided the *metta* chant in Pali from a Malaysian Buddhist monastery and gave me much help in understanding the *metta* practice. Sue Greer Lamie helped with chant intonations and provided copy explaining how to do the chanting. My daughter, Rebecca Bradshaw, first introduced me to IMS and also sparked my interest in doing intensive *metta* practice myself. I thank all of them. I also thank those who have trusted me to walk with them in their spiritual lives, for I have learned much from them.

I thank Michael Leach and John Eagleson of Crossroad Publishing Co. for their continuing support of my work.

Part I

Loving-Kindness

Chapter 1

TO LIVE WITHOUT FEAR
Understanding Loving-Kindness

T HIS BOOK is about an important teaching that both the Christ and the Buddha gave us — the need for universal, non-discriminating love for all others. It teaches a practice for being a kind and friendly presence in the world and for living without fear.

THE BUDDHA'S TEACHING ON UNIVERSAL LOVE

When one day some disciples came running to the Buddha in fear, he taught them how to live fearlessly among those who frightened them. The story has been carried down in commentaries to the Buddhist scriptures. It is alluded to in preliminary verses of praise that the elders put before the Buddha's *sutta* (sermon) teaching *metta,* or loving-kindness. The *sutta* itself is an early Buddhist scripture in the original Pali canon.

Here are the verses of praise that precede the sermon:

> Due to the glorious power of this teaching on Love,
> Spirits dare not create their frightful sights.
> One who diligently devotes oneself,
> Both day and night, to this practice
> Sleeps soundly and sees no nightmare when asleep.
> Oh, let us engage in this practice
> That has such advantages and noble attributes.[1]

The first teaching. Here is the story. The Buddha's
monks always spent the three months of each rainy season
in a fixed location doing intensive meditation practice. One
year some went together to a distant forest with some huge
trees under which they could take shelter. Some tree-demons
who lived there were displeased by the monks' presence and
decided to try to frighten them away. They harassed them
in various ways, often making very frightening visions and
noises at night.

Finally the monks could take it no longer, and they ran
back to the Buddha for help. The Buddha taught them
loving-kindness practice, telling them to radiate universal
love to all sentient beings everywhere. The monks went back
to the forest and obeyed the Buddha's instruction. The tree-
demons were so captivated by the love being sent them that
they ceased tormenting the monks and even began to serve
them.

The Buddha's way to overcome fear is so simple: practice
loving-kindness toward all beings. His teaching in the *Metta
Sutta* is strikingly similar to the Christian understanding of
agape love. As the Buddha said that love casts out fear, so
also Christian teachings say: "There is no fear in love. But
perfect love drives out fear.... One who fears is not made
perfect in love" (1 John 4:18).

The Buddha's sermon on *metta*. Let us look at the
Metta Sutta (sermon) from the *Sutta Nipata* in its entirety.
We will discuss different parts of it in both this chapter and
chapter 4.

One must be able, upright, perfectly upright,
Docilely teachable, gentle, and not conceited,
Easily satisfied and easily supported,
With few duties, and living very lightly,
With senses calmed, prudently wise, and not rude,
Not being covetous of other folks,
Abstaining from the ways that wise ones blame,

And this the thought that one should always hold:
"May beings all live happily and safe,
And may their hearts rejoice within themselves."
Whatever there may be with breath of life
Whether they be frail or very strong
Without exception, be they long or short
Or middle-sized, or be they big or small,
Or thick, or beings we have seen or those we have not seen,
Or whether they dwell far or they dwell near,
Those that are here, those seeking to be born.
Let no one bring about another's ruin,
And not despise in any way or place.
Let them not wish each other any ill
From provocation or from enmity.
Just as a mother at the risk of life
Loves and protects her child, her only child,
So one should cultivate this boundless love
To all that live in the whole universe.
One should radiate the boundless rays of love
Toward the entire world:
Above, below, and across without any obstruction
Without any malice or enmity.
And while one stands and while one walks and sits
Or one lies down still free from drowsiness
One should abide on this mindfulness.
This is the noblest living there is.
If, without falling into egoism,
One is virtuous and endowed with insight,
Discarding attachment to sense desires,
Never again will one be caught in the rounds of existence.[2]

THE POWER AND IMPORTANCE
OF LOVING-KINDNESS

The wisdom of love. The Buddha spoke of the wisdom of loving-kindness in the *Dhammapada* collection of sayings: "Hatred is never overcome by hatred; hatred is overcome only by love."[3] And Jesus said, "If you forgive others when they sin against you, your heavenly Father will also forgive you. But if you do not forgive others their sins, your Father will not forgive your sins" (Matt. 6:14–15). A well-developed habit of loving-kindness can rescue us when we are drawn toward animosity. The fruits of this practice also flow into our actions as generosity, caring, and service.

The Buddha told his monks: "Whatever kinds of worldly merit there are, all are not worth one sixteenth part of the heart-deliverance of loving-kindness; in shining and beaming and radiance the heart-deliverance of loving-kindness far excels them."[4]

Self-protection. The Buddha also emphasized the protection that loving-kindness can offer, saying:

> Monks, any monk who has not maintained in being and made much of the heart-deliverance of loving-kindness is readily ruined.... Any monk who maintains in being and makes much of the heart-deliverance of loving-kindness is not readily ruined.... So, monks, you should train in this way: The heart-deliverance of loving-kindness will be maintained in being and made much of by us, used as our vehicle, used as our foundation.... That is how you should train.[5]

The Buddha's persecutor, his jealous cousin Devadatta, once unloosed an enraged elephant to charge the Buddha in a narrow alley. The Buddha put all his monks behind him, and then began radiating *metta* to the elephant. As the elephant got nearer to the Buddha, it slowed. Finally, it stopped before the Buddha and knelt in homage. We, of course, are not the Buddha. One Buddhist teacher tells of sending *metta* to a dog of which he was afraid as he slowly approached it. The dog charged and bit him. The teacher says he realized that the *metta* sent the dog was not really genuine, but that he was trying to use it like a magic charm.

Helpfulness to others. Many people can see how *metta* practice helps us become more gentle and loving, and they acknowledge that this is a great benefit. But, they ask, does it really do anything for the beings to whom we send *metta*? The answer is: it depends. Qualities of both the sender and the receiver of *metta* determine how effective it is for the receiver. When we send *metta,* we should do so as whole-heartedly as we can, and then surrender the outcomes.

The more concentrated the sender is, the more penetrating is his or her focused mind. The more pure the mind of the sender is, the less it is obscured with the clutter of unwholesome states of mind that compete with *metta.* So purity and concentration of the sender increase the power of *metta.* The recipient's ability to receive depends upon his or her purity of mind and openness to receiving. Faith in the practice on the part of both increases its potency. This parallels Jesus' frequently telling people that their faith made it possible for them to receive his gifts.

THE RANGE OF LOVING-KINDNESS

The practice of *metta* enjoins an attitude of universal, non-discriminating friendliness and good will toward all beings with no exception. Several Buddhist *suttas* strongly make this point. However, when we practice *metta* intensively, we build our *metta* working with people of the gender to which we are not sexually attracted. We do not want to confound the feeling of *metta* with sexual interest. We also do not practice intensively on specific dead human beings.[6]

From the *Metta Sutta*. The *Metta Sutta,* which elaborates the practice of loving-kindness, gives a poetic list of those toward whom *metta* should be practiced:

Whatever there may be with breath of life
Whether they be frail or very strong
Without exception, be they long or short

Or middle-sized, or be they big or small,
Or thick, or beings we have seen or those we have not
    seen,
Or whether they dwell far or they dwell near,
Those that are here, those seeking to be born...
One should cultivate this boundless love
To all that live in the whole universe.[7]

This list includes the underprivileged and powerless of any society, such as women and minorities. It includes our next-door neighbors, but also our neighbors half-way around the world — be they Arab, Jew, Russian, or Chinese. It includes the elderly, the ill, the unborn, insects. It also includes those who wield power. Remember, the Buddha's original teaching on *metta* told his monks to extend it to beings who were creating trouble for them at that time.

It matters not how appealing or unappealing to us another being is; all are to be treated with the same loving attitude. "You have heard that it was said, 'Love your neighbor and hate your enemy.' But I tell you: Love your enemies and pray for those who persecute you, that you may be children of your Father in heaven. God causes the sun to rise on the evil and the good, and sends rain on the righteous and the unrighteous" (Matt. 5:43–45).

The second *Metta Sutta*. A teaching preached by Sariputta, one of the Buddha's chief disciples, is sometimes called the second *Metta Sutta*. "The heart-deliverance of loving-kindness is practiced with unspecified extension, with specified extension, and with directional extension."[8] The teaching then lists all the categories of beings to whom *metta* is sent in formal practice — specified and unspecified extension, which will be described in chapter 5. It also designates ten different directions to which *metta* should be sent. These also are explained in chapter 5.

The point of the list of all these beings and all these directions is that they are taken to cover all possible beings and all possible directions in which beings may be. So this teaching emphasizes the universality our *metta* must have and gives instructions on how to practice *metta* with that universality.

THE HEAVENLY ABODES, THE *BRAHMAVIHARA* PRACTICES

The word *brahmavihara* means "heavenly abode" or "home of the gods." It refers to the quality of mind of beings in the *brahma* realms, the highest type of conditioned existence in Buddhist cosmology. These beings rest deeply concentrated in very happy and positive states of mind, so deeply absorbed in them that nothing unpleasant can intrude into the mind. A very deep and subtle bliss dominates their existence.

Metta is the basic *brahmavihara* and includes the others. They are simply ways that *metta* is manifest in different situations.

Compassion. The second *brahmavihara* is *karuna* (kuh-roo'-nah), or compassion, the right attitude toward beings who are suffering. There is a specific practice for developing compassion, as there are for all *brahmaviharas*. Compassion helps us abide in the suffering of the whole, feeling with those who are suffering, and wanting to alleviate suffering when we encounter it.

Along with wisdom, compassion is one of the great wings of the Buddha's teachings. We could also say that it practices this beatitude: "Blessed are those who mourn, for they will be comforted" (Matt. 5:4).

Sympathetic joy. The third *brahmavihara* is the counterpart of compassion. *Mudita* (moo'-dee-tah), gladness or sympathetic joy, is taking satisfaction and delight in the good that others enjoy. It is the exact opposite of envy and jealousy. The main thing we are to be happy about for others is their spiritual advancement. With such gladness we practice the beatitude: "Blessed are those who hunger and thirst for righteousness, for they will be filled" (Matt. 5:6).

Equanimity. "Blessed are the peacemakers, for they will be called children of God" (Matt. 5:9). This quality of evenness of mind, of balance, of being able to maintain peace in all circumstances, is *upekkha* (oo-pek'-kah) or equanimity, the fourth *brahmavihara*. It is especially important when other people's behavior does not conform to our wishes for them.[9]

THE UNITIVE METAPHYSICS OF LOVING-KINDNESS

A unitive metaphysics underlies the love commandments of all the world's great spiritualities. This metaphysics of unity is described in various symbolic ways — such as all people's being children of the same God, members of the same Mystical Body, or flowing from the same Source. The commandment of love for others rests upon the belief that somehow, in our deepest being, our fates are inextricably intertwined, as intertwined as are the fates of my heart and my liver. Too much damage to either affects the other adversely. A sane person would not allow one hand to chop off the other because it would hurt the organic unity of the body to which both hands belong. So also a person who understands is unable to harm any other person. Harm done to anyone is harm done to oneself, to the larger whole encompassing both.

Such a unitive attitude indeed seems one that the great religious leaders and founders intended for their followers to hold; this is clearly what Jesus the Christ and Gotama the Buddha taught. However, they urged a unity that is a bond of love and mutual affirmation — not one forged from forced uniformity of creed, doctrine, or practice. "God is love. Whoever lives in love lives in God, and God in them" (John 4:16). When we recognize that we all live together in the love that God is, this attitude reflects in the loving-kindness with which we treat all beings.

AN EXAMPLE FROM TODAY'S WORLD

The stories of two Mideast hostages show clearly the difference between loving-kindness and its absence. A British hostage released in 1990 was asked if he wanted revenge on his captors. He replied that he did not, for such attitudes are self-maiming and he did not wish to maim himself in that way. Similar understanding was shown by the well-known Terry Waite in a post-hostage interview. He reported that a rule he had for himself during his captivity was to feel no bitterness and no self-pity. Both of these men understand well how attitudes opposed to love only create more suffering for us when we are already suffering and inflict more general suffering on the world as a whole.

Contrast their attitudes with that of an American hostage released in 1991. When asked about revenge, he said he could not get it out of his mind. He felt that his captors should be chained for forty years, the cumulative amount of time he and fellow hostages were chained. What differences in freedom and happiness in the minds of each of these hostages, and in the atmosphere the presence of each is likely to create! It is so evident that we need not comment further.

IN CLOSING

Both the Christ and the Buddha told us that our love must be universal, must be extended to all without exception — even to those who do wrong and create suffering for others. Remember, the *Dhammapada* quotes the Buddha as saying: "Hatred is never overcome by hatred; hatred is overcome only by love."[10] And the Christ told us never to return evil for evil, but to do good to those who would harm us in any way. "Love your enemies, do good to them, and lend to them without expecting to get anything back" (Luke 6:3). Well-deserved is peace, protection, and serenity in the lives of those who move our world toward healing by living in such loving-kindness. May we all be moved to so live.

Chapter 2

BURNING UP YOUR SUPPORT

The Torment of Anger

ANGER, a form of hatred, is diametrically opposed to *metta*. It is *metta*'s major obvious enemy. The *Visuddhimagga* states unequivocally, "It is not possible to practice loving-kindness and feel anger simultaneously."[1]

The *Visuddhimagga* recommends reflecting on the flaws in anger and malice, and on the advantages of patience, before starting *metta* practice.[2] The great Burmese meditation master Mahasi Sayadaw also encouraged this. He believed that many modern people make anger a friend and even come to enjoy it in spite of the suffering it inflicts on both self and others.[3] Examining its faults helps clear the way to *metta*.

NATURE OF ANGER

Buddhist understandings. Hatred is one of the three roots of all immoral action in Buddhist psychology, along with greed and delusion. Because of this, Buddhist thought has no place for notions like "just war," "righteous indignation," or anger "needed" to get things done. Necessary actions can be spurred by other motives; we do not need anger to propel us.

Hatred includes many kinds and degrees of aversion, anger, annoyance, animosity, and ill will. It has a ferocious character. It burns up its own support — that is, the mind and body that experience it. It is caused by encountering something unpleasant or not liked, and it manifests itself in trying to "persecute" the unpleasant object.

All hatred puts an aggressive and rough coloration on the mind. It defiles the person feeling it, who is repelled by some object. The mental state of hatred becomes a full action when it brings the wish that another being suffer harm or affliction. When we overcome hatred, we can relinquish resentment and anger.

Christian perspectives. Rage is one of the acts of sinful nature incompatible with life in the spirit (Gal. 5:20). "Love never wrongs the neighbor" (Rom. 13:10). "Those who claim to be in the light but hate a brother [or sister] are still in darkness... and walk around in shadows; they do not know where they are going, because the darkness has blinded their eyes" (1 John 2:9–11).

Holding onto anger is clearly incompatible with Christian living. "But now you must rid yourselves of all these: anger, quick temper, malice, slanderous insults" (Col. 3:8). "We are to be slow to anger, for anger does not fulfill God's justice" (James 1:19–20). St. Paul was greatly distressed that members of the early Christian community were taking each other to court rather than settling their differences gently (1 Cor. 6:6ff.).

The message is clear. "In your anger do not sin. Do not let the sun go down while you are still angry.... Get rid of all bitterness, rage and anger, harsh words, and slander, along with every kind of malice. Be kind and compassionate to one another, forgiving each other" (Eph. 4:26, 31–32). "In everything you do, act without grumbling or arguing" (Phil. 2:14).

UNDERSTANDING ANGER

Anger has two major components. An angry person feels attacked in some way. There is also some sense of loss.

Attack. One of three kinds of "attack" might precede anger. Direct attack is obvious. Someone hits you, ridicules you, lies about you, steals from you, molests you, or so on. You have been attacked and you know it.

Indirect attack is less easily recognized. Such things as hot weather, overcrowding, a flat tire, back pain, a long line, or a lost object are examples. We might deny feeling attacked by such things, but at some level they assault our being. And we frequently react with irritation, annoyance, or outright anger. Any big-city police officer knows that overcrowded living conditions on a hot summer night are a potential tinderbox.

"Imaginary" attack is even harder to recognize. These are events taken personally because of touchiness, egoism, rigidity, or other conditions of psychological ill health. Perhaps your spouse forgets to kiss you, and you feel demeaned. Or someone desecrates a symbol you value, like burning a flag, and you are enraged. Maybe someone acts contrary to your values — has an abortion or engages in a homosexual act — and you become very punitive.

Some people cannot forgive their parents for having had ordinary human flaws. Other people take general remarks personally. Someone once raged at me for ten minutes when I exhorted a retreat group to use their remaining time well; she had taken it as a personal scolding. In these imaginary attacks, nobody is "out to get us," but we react as if they were.

Loss. What we lose in direct attack is often obvious. In indirect attack, we may lose comfort, convenience, time, control over circumstances, a sense of self-sufficiency, or similar values. In imaginary attacks, personal power, self-esteem, feeling loved or respected, or even some sense of our integrity as a person may feel lost. Psychological woundedness makes us unable to maintain these supportive states unless other people behave exactly as we wish.

Self-deception. When we are angry, most of our energy is usually directed outward. We dwell upon what annoys us or on the offensive features of somebody or something. This causes anger to increase whether the causes are real, exaggerated, or plain delusional. All anger can be considered temporary insanity!

Anger is not always overt and apparent. We very easily deceive ourselves. When angry at someone we fear, we might "take it out" on a safe target — like kicking the dog. We also may "project" the anger. This works just like a movie projector; the picture in the projector is seen as if it were on the wall. We see our anger as if it were coming from another person. If you ever feel a friend is annoyed with you, but don't know why, check to see how you may be annoyed with your friend.

We also may act sugary sweet to disguise anger, and then believe our own lie! Parents sometimes engage in this tactic, which we call reaction formation, and make their children miserable by overly protecting them. Some people express anger by obstructing things; we call this passive aggression. Frequent lateness, "messing up" unwanted tasks, or leaving personal belongings where they annoy others may be passive aggression.

Finally, we might decide that our anger is for the good of another. We rationalize with such notions as "She needed someone to take her down a peg or two" or "I only told him for his own good." In all these classical "defense mechanisms," we add self-deception to the anger.

Trying to repair attack and loss. The common angry reaction is lashing out in counterattack. We might try to bring the attacker down, to restructure the environment forcefully, or to "barrier" ourselves off emotionally. Some people even believe it unhealthy not to express anger openly. While it *is* unhealthy to deceive ourselves about being angry, overt expression of anger is not needed. Acting out feeds and increases anger.

Other reactions are more appropriate for spiritual seekers. Direct attack calls for forgiveness — for our own sake! We need not continue to accept abuse, however. Indirect attack calls most clearly for patience. Imaginary attack invites us to withdraw our demands and expectations of others and to respect their freedom of conscience and personal rights as we want ours respected.

WRETCHEDNESS OF ANGER

As a metaphor for a mind filled with anger, the Buddha said: "Imagine a bowl of water, heated on a fire, boiling up and bubbling over. If a person with good eyesight were to look at the reflection of their own face in it, they could not know or see it as it really is."[4]

Seven ill effects of anger. From the Buddha: "Seven things gratifying and helpful to an enemy befall one who is angry.... What are the seven?"

First, angry people look ugly. "Looks betray the sulkiness of some dim smoky smoldering glow." Next, they are in pain. "One suffers as if seared by fire." When we harbor resentment, *we* suffer the heat, obsessing, and tension — not the person we are resenting. Sometimes our minds perversely seem to enjoy this suffering.

Third, we may lose benefits from making mistakes. "This fury does so cloud the mind...that...an angry person no meaning knows; no angry person sees an idea, so wrapped in darkness, as if blind, is one whom anger dogs." Fourth, we may lose property if we act on anger in ways that make us legally liable.

Fifth, we fall into disrepute and disgrace. "The wrath and rage that madden one, gain that one a name of ill repute." People are not well-disposed toward those who show such lack of self-control. They feel they cannot be trusted, and are not safe to be around. Sixth, we lose friends. "Friends, relatives and kin will seek to shun [an angry person], keeping their distance." Being around angry people is unpleasant. People keep their lives happier by avoiding such persons.

Seventh, we set up possible future tenure in hell, which is a temporary state in Buddhist thought. Jesus and the Buddha gave the same teaching on this, "Anyone who is angry with another will be subject to judgment,...who holds another in contempt will be in danger of the fire of hell" (Matt. 5:22). All these forms of self-inflicted suffering do to us only what an enemy might wish for us![5]

Reprehensibility of anger. The Buddha explained that when we hate, we are a prey to hate and are obsessed by it.[6] He cautioned that hatred can even lead people to killing their parents, or themselves.

"When one is depraved through hate, when one is over-whelmed and infatuated by hate, then one thinks and plans for one's own harm, one thinks and plans for the harm of others,...and one experiences in the mind suffering and grief. One also leads a bad life in deeds, words and thoughts, and one does not understand, as it really is, one's own welfare, nor the welfare of others."[7] When hate has been abandoned, we do none of these things.

OVERCOMING ANGER

"Hatred is more reprehensible, but easier to remove" than greed or delusion.[8] This is because it is such a painful state in itself, while the other two are not. Asking pardon of those we have wronged through hate makes it even easier to over-come its effects in us than is overcoming flaws like conceit and greed.

Relinquishing negativity. "This person abused me, beat me, and overcame and plundered me. Wrapped up in such thought, one will never appease hatred....Stripped bare of such thoughts, hatred is quickly appeased. Never by ha-tred is hatred appeased, but only by love. This is an eternal law."[9] The Buddha's teachings clearly tell us that reflecting on another's bad points only feeds anger. If we truly want to overcome it, we must think of all the good we can about others. St. Paul echoed this: "Do not be overcome by evil, but conquer evil with good" (Rom. 12:31).

Five ways to remove grudges. The Buddha's teachings are full of practical advice. He explained five good ways to remove resentments.[10] First maintain loving-kindness toward one toward whom you are annoyed. For those who practice loving-kindness, as taught in this book, this is not so hard as it sounds.

If you cannot do this, maintain compassion. Angry people are suffering. When someone is angry with you, remember that that person is feeling attacked and experiencing loss. Elsewhere the Buddha said, "Understanding another's angry mood, you can help that one clear it and find peace."[11] A third technique is also fostered by doing *brahmavihara* practice. We become an impartial observer of what is happening, staying in onlooking equanimity.

We also can forget and ignore provocation. Reacting to anger or ill treatment often only increases it. If we *must* stop another's actions, we can act without the heat of anger. Finally, we can think of the ultimate effects on the other person. Those who live in hatred develop a heart that draws suffering to itself. Jesus also said this: "All who live by the sword will be destroyed by it" (Matt. 26–52).

Gift giving. Giving a gift to, and accepting a gift from, someone who angers us helps overcome animosity. Psychological studies confirm this ancient wisdom from the Buddhist tradition. One psychologist taught angry students to practice doing good for their antagonists. Within three months, many hostile relationships had turned friendly. Between 65 percent and 80 percent of either friendly or hostile approaches drew the same response from the other person.[12]

Even if another person is incapable of responding to such goodness, it still affects the person doing it.

REFLECTIONS TO OVERCOME ANGER

Sometimes, try as might want, we cannot bring ourselves to do what we know overcomes anger. The *Visuddhimagga* offers reflections to overcome anger.[13] Some of them repeat the Buddha's direct teachings. Working with any of these can help us become more willing.

First, we can reflect on the beauty and value of patience. We can also consider the Buddha's teaching, given above, on how anger feeds into what enemies might wish for us. Are we not simply filling their desires for us if we let them upset us?

The Buddha said "to repay angry people in kind is worse than to be angry first";[14] we allow someone of whom we do not approve to dictate our conduct. When we are angry, we respond to someone with behavior that we have judged wrong in that person. Is it reasonable to follow the example of someone we consider to be in the wrong?

We can also willingly relinquish negative thought about the other and replace it with some good thought about the person. Nobody is totally bad. If we truly find nothing we can approve, we can compassionately realize that this person is creating continuing suffering for him- or herself.

We must realize that, by themselves, others can hurt only the physical body. We must cooperate for harm to be done to the mind. Why should we please antagonists by choosing to suffer in ways they cannot make us suffer without our help?

We often give up good things to accomplish other aims important to us. Since we are able to do this, why not give up anger, which offers us no benefit and only draws down disaster? When we hold onto anger, we make patience, compassion, and kindness impossible. Why choose to cling to something that destroys morality and virtue?

Although we want to make someone else miserable when we are angry, we cannot be sure of accomplishing this. However, we know we make ourselves miserable. How intelligent is that?

When we commit wrong acts, we are engaging in vice. Can we really find any justification for choosing that? When we let anger determine our actions, we have made ourselves a slave to anger. Do we want anger to be our ruler?

Any person who wronged us no longer exists. Just as we are constantly changing, so also is the other person. The one we are now faced with is not the same as the one who made us angry. So, what are angry at?

Since we must cooperate for the anger of another to affect us, we are a "partner in the crime." Why should we be angry at only the other person? This is not suggesting that we should also be angry at ourselves, but that the anger itself is foolish.

AND NOW...

The first step out of anger is patience. Patience makes *metta*, gentle friendliness, possible. In the next chapter, we discuss patience, then look at the benefits of loving-kindness.

Chapter 3

TOWARD HEART-DELIVERANCE
The Grace of Patience

PATIENCE comes from developing the ability to endure and to tolerate environmental discomforts, unpleasant speech, unwanted actions of others, and so on. It is one of five major methods of self-control by discipline in Buddhist psychology; the other four are morality, mindfulness, wisdom, and effort.[1]

When we are patient, we allow ourselves to be worked on. The work on us sometimes comes from the environment, sometimes other people, and sometimes from within ourselves. We accept any kind of inconvenience as fodder for our spiritual work. We willingly endure necessary suffering. We are the seed fallen on good ground that will "bring forth fruit with patience" (Luke 8:15). Thus, we can "glory in tribulations, knowing that trials bring patience" (Rom. 5:3).

Patience, however, does not mean being a doormat and encouraging others in bad behavior. It is not incompatible with taking gentle corrective action when appropriate. Doing this can be a kindness to others. When we become truly patient, we can trust our discernment. We know when simply to accept what happens and when circumstances ought be changed.

THE NATURE OF PATIENCE

The Buddha defined patience: "And what, monks, is the way of patience? If scolded, one does not scold in return; if insulted, one does not insult in return; if abused, one does not abuse in return."[2] Patience is one of the *paramis* (virtues) that the Buddha developed to a very high degree in his aspiration to become a Buddha. All his disciples are also to develop these qualities, which read like the list of Christian fruits of the Holy Spirit.

The Buddha also said that patience is "great good fortune," one form of the greatest blessings we can have. "Reverence, humility, contentment, and gratitude, to hear the teachings at helpful times,...patience, the soft answer, the sight of those who are controlled, and spiritual talk in good times — this is the greatest blessing."[3]

For Christians, patience is one of the fruits of the Holy Spirit in which we are to clothe ourselves (Gal. 5:22), and "in patience, you possess your soul" (Luke 21:19). It is also how we live following Jesus who said, "Take my yoke upon your shoulders and learn from me, for I am gentle and humble of heart" (Matt. 11:29). St. Paul enjoined us to live in patience: "Live a life worthy of the calling you have received with perfect humility, meekness, and patience, bearing with one another lovingly" (Eph. 4:1–2).

VALUE AND NEED OF PATIENCE

Patience in life. Patience has been called the most noble virtue because it makes us able to tolerate things that could easily draw out bad behavior. The Buddha said, "No greater thing exists than patience."[4] This state is considered the one most contrary to anger. That makes it a necessary basis for *metta* to ripen; without patience, we are incapable of *metta*.

Patience also is necessary to be moral, to be able to concentrate the mind, and to develop spiritual wisdom. A Buddhist saying teaches that patience will carry us to *nib-

bana, the Buddhist Ultimate Reality. This is like saying that patience makes us able to know God.

The letter of James to the churches describes patience as a way to build community:

> Be patient, then, brothers, until the Lord's coming. See how farmers...patiently wait during the autumn and spring rains. You too be patient with a steady heart, because the Lord's coming is near. Don't grumble against each other...or you will be judged....As an example of patience in the face of suffering, take the prophets who spoke in the name of the Lord. As you know we call blessed those who have endured. You have heard of Job's perseverance and have seen what the compassionate and merciful Lord finally brought about. (James 5:7–11)

James also encouraged patience for personal surrender to God. "Know that being tested brings patience. Let patience work perfectly in you, that you may be whole and entire, lacking nothing" (James 1:34). St. Paul instructed Titus to teach thus: "Tell them not to speak evil of anyone or be quarrelsome. They must be forbearing and display a perfect courtesy toward all" (Titus 3:2).

Patience in meditation practice. Patience is needed to be faithful to spiritual practice. We all have times when we are disinclined to our spiritual work or when it feels distinctly unpleasant. We must be willing to endure such unwanted conditions if we want to persevere. If we add mental complaining to these situations, we increase the suffering involved. This mental stiffness can produce tension in the body that makes the entire situation increasingly worse. Then we become impatient with the new suffering that has been created.[5] We get into a downward spiraling that can end with our quitting. On the other hand, when we are patient, we can be with the situation for as long as it lasts and will eventually come out beyond it.

We must also be patient with our progress in practice. The discipline of meditation is hard work. It is not called practice without reason. You do not expect to play Mozart sonatas when you first sit down at a piano, or to shoot baskets consistently when you first begin basketball practice. You also must not expect meditation to be easy initially.

Although meditation can eventually produce great relaxation of both body and mind, that is not the starting point. We all begin by contending with a mind that seems completely unwilling to stay put. Often our bodies are either sleepy or restless when we try to meditate. We may feel like we are completely unfit for meditation. Sometimes we start practice with very unreal expectations about what we will experience and how rapidly or easily practice will go for us. Without realizing it, we are "demanding" particular outcomes.

The Buddha said that spiritual practice can be either fast or slow and either easy or difficult. While we would all prefer fast and easy practice, we almost always get a different combination! As we settle into the reality of spiritual practice, we would be lost without patience. St. Teresa of Avila said that we "calmly and wisely must understand that one does not deal well with God by force."[6]

ENDURING ABUSE

The teaching of Jesus. "If someone strikes you on one cheek, turn the other also to them. If someone takes your coat, do not stop them from taking your shirt. Give to everyone who asks of you, and if anyone takes what belongs to you, do not demand it back" (Luke 6:29–30). Jesus demonstrated such long-suffering when he was being arrested. "One of them struck the servant of the high priest, cutting off his right ear. But Jesus answered. 'Enough of this.' And he touched the man's ear and healed him" (Luke 22:50–51). Jesus' attitude of forgiving patience is evident throughout the passion story. Its final proof is the dying prayer for his executioners, "Father, forgive them for they do not know what they do" (Luke 23:34).

Jesus' entire life also modeled for us patience that knew when to accept without reaction, and when action was needed. He often grieved for others who mistreated him, knowing that they were creating misery for themselves. Yet he willingly challenged those who tried to impose unfair religious burdens on the people and whose questions to him were hypocritical. Our patience must be wise like that of Jesus. We must not become vindictive when harmed, but also must not encourage others in wrongdoing by failing to challenge behavior that ought be stopped.

St. Paul told us to "be patient in affliction" (Rom. 12:12), and said that he did not stop praying that the followers of Jesus be "long-suffering with joyfulness" (Col. 1:11). Elsewhere he taught: "Clothe yourselves with heartfelt mercy, with kindness, humility, meekness, and patience. Bear with one another. Forgive whatever grievances you have against one another" (Col. 3:12–13). Even more directly, he said "Never repay injury with injury....Do not avenge yourselves" (Rom 12:17, 19).

The teaching of the Buddha. The Buddha taught that there is "no peace higher than forbearance."[7] When someone had abused the monk Phagguna, the Buddha said to him: "If anyone should abuse you to your face,...strike you with fist or hurl clods of earth at you, or beat you with a stick, or give you a blow with a sword — yet must you...train yourself: 'My heart will be unwavering. No evil word will I send forth. I will abide compassionate of others' welfare, of kindly heart, without resentment.'"[8]

The Buddha went even further: "Though robbers or vile people should with a two-handed saw carve you in pieces limb by limb, yet if the mind of any one of you should be angered at this, such a one does not follow my teaching."[9] This "parable of the saw" is widely cited as an example of the extent to which patience should be carried. In the crucifixion, Jesus clearly modeled this kind of patience for us.

An annoyed man once came and heaped abuse on the Buddha. The Buddha then asked him if he ever received visits from friends and relatives. When the man said he did, the Buddha asked if he offered them food. When the man again replied in the affirmative, the Buddha asked what happens when they don't accept these gifts. The man said that his unaccepted gifts still belong to him. The Buddha then said, "So it is here, brahmin. The abuse, the scolding, the reviling you hurl at us who do not abuse or scold or revile, we do not accept from you. It all belongs to you.... It is all yours."[10]

The *Jataka* tales, stories of previous lives of the Buddha, describe many instances in which he showed great patience when suffering was inflicted on him. In one, when an ill-minded king asked him what he taught, he answered that he taught patience. The king then flogged him with thorns and cut off his hands and feet.[11] Such stories mirror the patience of Jesus; both he and the Buddha responded to provocation without anger.

Many stories of Buddhist monks and nuns describe great patient forbearing. One of my favorites is about when bandits were terrorizing some small villages. Most villagers fled at their approach, but one monk remained in his monastery. When the chief bandit heard this, he was greatly angered. Cornering the monk, he asked, "Don't you know that you are looking at someone who could run you through with a sword without blinking an eye?" The monk replied, "Don't you know you are looking at someone who can be run through by a sword without blinking an eye?" The story says that this converted the bandit, who himself became a great saint.

REFLECTION ON THE BENEFITS OF
LOVING-KINDNESS

Once the grosser forms of anger have been conquered and some degree of patience has ripened, we can more easily develop loving-kindness. Non-anger and patience themselves bring great blessings, but the Buddha also specifically listed additional direct advantages of *metta*.

He said, "Monks, when the heart-deliverance of loving-kindness is maintained in being, made much of, used as one's vehicle, used as one's foundation,...then eleven blessings can be expected."[12] The specific advantages that come to those who practice loving-kindness are grouped below into several categories. Much in our own lives supports the Buddha's list of the benefits of love.

Sleep and dreams. We who practice and cherish *metta* go to sleep easily, and sleep in sound comfort. We also wake feeling refreshed, comfortable, and happy. The *Visuddhimagga* says, "Instead of waking uncomfortably, groaning and yawning and turning over as others do, [one] wakes comfortably without contortions, like a lotus opening."[13] People who wake reluctantly and need time to "get going" should appreciate this blessing. *Metta* practitioners also dream no evil dreams, but have pleasant and happy dreams.

Have we not all experienced that nothing begets peace like a loving attitude? If we are harboring ill-will within, it not only obsesses us during the day, but works its way into our dreams, disturbing sleep. We can "sleep like a baby" when our minds reflect the innocence of a baby's mind.

Being loved. Practicing *metta* makes us dear to other human beings. When we truly love, we cause no harm to others; this draws their affection and respect. What may sound like an overworked cliché is easily proven true in our dealings with other beings. We need simply reflect on the type of people we prefer to be around.

Metta also makes us dear to non-human beings. The power of love to attract even animals is seen in such people as St. Francis of Assisi and other saints in many different spiritual traditions. Adults may sometimes be fooled, but young children and animals easily sense when a truly loving attitude is behind others' behavior toward them, and respond accordingly.

Protection. *Devas* (lower gods, or angels) protect *metta* practitioners. Just as some Christians believe that angels have ministered to them at times of need, Buddhists report such loving care from *devas,* beings described similarly to how Christians understand angels. *Devas* are also said to be strongly drawn to people who practice generosity and morality.[14]

No fire or poison or weapon can harm loving people. Buddhists believe that the quality of our minds determines what happens to us, and Buddhist lore is full of stories illustrating this claim.[15] The mind of one who practices *metta* has earned much protection. Love protects those who manifest it, and when we are all love, there is no unprotected place in our lives. As St. John told us, perfect love casts out all fear (1 John 4:18); protection means freedom from fear.

Concentration and calm. The mind must be stabilized and calm to do any kind of meditation. *Metta* makes us easily able to concentrate our minds, and thus do spiritual practice. The mind of a loving person does not churn with envies, resentments, vengeance, restlessness, or other painful emotions. It also does not drown in sluggishness, drowsiness, or boredom.

The quality of our minds reflects in our faces. One sage said that everyone over forty is responsible for how his or her face looks; it reveals the character we have been developing. Practicing *metta* keeps our facial expression serene.

Happy death. Death often occurs with both physical and mental pain; sometimes the mind also is very foggy and unclear. *Metta* lets us die without falling into confusion. The teachings say that we pass away easily as if falling asleep. Love brings clarity and simplicity to life, and this benefit stays with us at the time of death. "Whoever loves others lives in the light and there is nothing in them to make them stumble" (1 John 2:10).

Buddhists say that if we are not yet pure enough to "die into" *nibbana* (we could say: to "see" God), we will be reborn in the higher heavens if we practice *metta*. This is like a less arduous purgatory. Both Buddhist and Christian scriptures remind us that what we sow is what we will reap. Those who sow seeds of love will get love in return. "Everyone who loves has been born of God and knows God" (1 John 4:7).

FURTHER PREPARATION

In the next chapter we look at qualities needed to practice *metta*. We will also study the Buddha's teachings on discerning true and false friendship.

Chapter 4

REJOICING HEARTS
Being Able to Practice
Loving-Kindness

ALTHOUGH we want to be truly loving, we realize it is easier said than done. However, we can cultivate characteristics that both Christian and Buddhist scriptures say help us to love. We can also do specific practices that encourage a loving attitude.

THOSE ABLE TO BE LOVINGLY KIND

A New Testament understanding. St. Paul gave a well-known Christian description of how *agape* persons behave:

This love of which I speak is slow to lose patience — it looks for a way of being constructive. It is not possessive; it is neither anxious to impress nor does it cherish inflated ideas of its own importance.

Love has good manners and does not pursue selfish advantage. It is not touchy. It does not keep account of evil or gloat over the wickedness of other people. On the contrary, it is glad with all good [people] when truth prevails.

Love knows no limit to its endurance, no end to its trust, no fading of its hope; it can outlast anything. It is, in fact, the one thing that still stands when all else has fallen." (1 Cor. 13:4–8, Phillips).

A description from Buddhist scriptures. The *Metta Sutta* describes an amazingly similar picture of this loving stance:

> One must be able, upright, perfectly upright,
> Docilely teachable, gentle, and not conceited,
> Easily satisfied and easily supported,
> With few duties, and living very lightly,
> With senses calmed, prudently wise, and not rude,
> Not being covetous of other folks,
> Abstaining from the ways that wise ones blame,
> And this the thought that one should always hold:
> "May beings all live happily and safe,
> And may their hearts rejoice within themselves."[1]

Summary. Both traditions tell us that loving people are patient and not caught up in the bustle of too many activities. They try to be constructive, and hence are teachable and easy to speak to. They are not greedy but live simply, and they are thrifty and easily satisfied. Not eager to impress others, they are straightforward and do not hold inflated opinions of themselves. They have good manners and are mild in dealing with others. They do not pursue selfish advantage, nor try to possess or control other people. They avoid conduct that wise people blame.

They do not keep count of evil or gloat over wickedness, but are truly happy about others' good fortune. They want no one to despise others or wish them any ill. They are glad when truth prevails and want all beings to rejoice in their hearts at all times. Their endurance knows no limit; they are not moved by enmity or provocation and wish no others to be so moved. Their trust, hope, and love have no end; at all times, in all places, and in all activities, they abide in loving-kindness.

Probably very few people alive today possess all these qualities to a high degree, but they are helpful guidelines for us. To the extent we develop such qualities in our speech and behavior, our hearts become more loving. And, as we do *metta* practice for a loving heart, these qualities grow in us. So a mutual interdependence exists between our meditation practice of loving-kindness and the behavior choices we make.

ANALYSIS OF NEEDED QUALITIES

This teaching about the qualities we must have for *metta* comes directly from the Buddha's words. He told us that they are prerequisites for *metta*. Let us discuss them, relying to some extent on Mahasi Sayadaw's work.[2]

Ability to practice. We must be capable of doing practice. Understanding the advantages of *metta* practice (chapter 3) helps us be able. We also must be firmly moral. Buddhist teachings say that without morality we cannot concentrate our minds enough for spiritual practice. The mind will constantly be drawn to guilt, shame, and remorse as we recall wrong behavior.

We also need enough faith in the practice to willingly put time into it. Faith rests on the testimony of others initially, but as practice brings results in our lives, faith grows. We must persevere to be successful. Little progress is made if we practice only when the whim hits us.

Honesty. We must be upright and honest. First is simple frankness and straightforwardness. Beyond not lying, simple honesty means not pretending to possess qualities we do not have. We make no claim to virtue or accomplishment that is not true.

For *metta*, we need even more radically complete honesty — perfect uprightness. We acknowledge our faults to get help in correcting them. We are willing for the spiritual teacher to know anything that is useful in guiding us. Those unwilling to acknowledge the truth of their own condition are not well-suited to *metta* practice.

Teachableness. We must also be docile and disposed to compliance. We Westerners often have trouble accepting that sometimes another knows more about something than we do, or that our best interests rest in doing what we are told rather than as we see fit. People who cannot accept benevolent advice, or who react badly when a suggestion is made to them, find spiritual practice difficult. Some people even become angry when a teacher points out unpleasant truths; this is a great hindrance to *metta!*

Gentleness. We must be mild with others; a curt and abrupt attitude works against developing *metta*. While *metta* practice increases our gentle friendliness to others, we must also not contradict kindness in our behavior. This includes not being conceited. A conceited person constantly compares self with others, a divisive and separating practice, which is not gentle and contradicts the bonding of *metta*.

Contentment. To practice *metta* we must be easily satisfied. The greed of constantly hankering after what we do not have impairs the concentration needed for *metta* practice. Living lightly, with few needs, makes this easier. Once we become accustomed to a simple life style, we realize that multiplying needs and desires unnecessarily distract us.

Few duties. Not having many demanding duties also helps spiritual practice. Busy people can live a spiritual life, but they must find some time to set duties aside. For this reason, some people make retreats regularly. When we put ourselves where the duties simply cannot find us, we can then concentrate on spiritual work.

Needless to say, some duties should not be shelved. We must meet necessary responsibilities to which we have committed ourselves. My annual three-month retreats did not begin until after my last child left home, although earlier I made shorter retreats after arranging for my children's care.

Calmness and prudence. Learning to stay calm greatly helps *metta* develop. This requires keeping the senses under control and being in a recollected attitude. When we allow ourselves to be pulled around by what we see and hear, we easily become restless or even agitated. Then we cannot respond in the most helpful ways for both ourselves and others.

Wise prudence means being able to discern well. We must understand which are helpful behaviors and choices and which are not. We then can choose to act in ways that foster our aims and allow loving-kindness to be fruitful.

Freedom from rudeness. Rudeness can be physical, verbal, or mental. All harm us. Simple good manners is a kindness to others. Unwillingness to be considerate is not conducive to a truly loving heart. This means we must refrain from doing and saying some things that we feel drawn to do or say.

Mental rudeness is letting ourselves "delight" in thinking ill about others. Since *metta* is fostered by seeing good in others, mental rudeness makes it more difficult to feel *metta*. Mahasi Sayadaw also includes here thinking disrespectful thoughts about people worthy of respect.[3] It is so easy to let envy or resentment color our relationships with worthy people!

Freedom from wrong attachment. In Buddhist psychology, the near enemy of any state of mind is one that outwardly looks like that state, while it actually works against it. Greediness in relationships is the "near enemy" of *metta*. Excessive attachment to other people hinders its development. The notion of co-dependence captures this understanding well. Co-dependent people think they are very loving, while they are really only trying to make themselves indispensable to others or to bind others to them. They use "love" for self-centered purposes.

Avoiding blameworthy behavior.   Not doing blameworthy actions begins with simple morality, but has a social
reference. We not only avoid behaviors we ourselves judge to
be wrong, but also actions that wise people consider scan-
dalous or wrong. This does not mean we always bow to
public opinion regarding our choices. However, we must
willingly listen to those who may be wiser, kinder, holier than
we are. This is a hard teaching for a nation as individualistic
and unwilling to respect "elders" as we are!

OTHER AIDS TO DEVELOPING *METTA*

The nearest cause of *metta* is seeing good in others. This
means that *metta* most easily arises when we can see good
in another. A major obstacle to feeling gentle friendliness
toward others is a habit of seeing bad in others, of being sensitive to what is wrong rather than what is right. We can train
ourselves to look for good by simply practicing it. The evan-
gelist John tells us this is a necessary self-training. "Those
who do not love their brothers and sisters, whom they have
seen, cannot love God, whom they have not seen" (1 John
4:20).

Thinking of the common human desire to be happy is
another helpful practice. Sometimes we have trouble seeing
good in others because we don't approve of how they seek
happiness. When we reflect on our own lives, we know that
we seek satisfaction where we think we can find it — for
example, in sensory pleasure, achievement, relationships, or
spiritual practice. If we understand our own wishes, we can
realize that other human beings have the same basic wishes
for themselves.

Putting the best possible interpretation on another's behavior also helps. We truly cannot know the motives behind
most of what other people do. If we believe we understand
their actions, we are likely to be seriously wrong. Jesus
warned us about judging: "Do not judge, or you too will be
judged. For in the same way you judge others, you will be

judged, and with the measure you use, it will be measured to you" (Matt. 7:1–2). We can neutralize this habit of judging or evaluating others. We can look for the best possible explanation for what they are doing and tell ourselves to accept this understanding.

Finally, an almost fool-proof way to develop tender feelings for others is to do something good for them. Mahasi Sayadaw considered it "essential to do good to others, and by doing so, the act of developing mindfulness on loving-kindness may be said to be genuinely effective."[4] When we do a favor for someone, we are investing in that person. We humans tend to protect our investments.

Sending *metta* to others is one way to invest in them. When our hearts are too hard to do this, doing a favor for someone can open the heart and make *metta* possible. Jesus assures us this effort will be worthwhile. "Give and it will be given to you; good measure, pressed down, shaken together, running over, will be put into your lap. For the measure you give will be the measure you get back" (Luke 6:38).

FRIENDSHIP FALSE AND TRUE

Metta has been called "gentle friendliness." The Buddha knew that not all that looks like friendship is true friendship. He gave specific guidelines to help us sort out true from false friends. They offer a good test of ourselves as a friend, as well as suggesting how to recognize friends who truly support our own greatest good. The Hebrew Bible (Old Testament) has similar passages.

False friends. The Buddha described several types of false friends, who are foes masquerading as friends.[5] First are the out-and-out robbers. These people take from you what they want to take. They try to get much by giving little and do their duty to you out of fear. They follow you for their own gain only.

Some false friends are good at words. They talk about

their own past deeds and promise that you can expect great future things from them. However, they merely ingratiate themselves with empty words. They are not around when needed and offer excuses by pointing to their own ill luck. Jesus understood those who love God in this way, saying that merely crying out "Lord, Lord" is not enough (Matt. 7:21).

A third type is smooth-tongued; such people are double-faced. They comply* in evil deeds, but are not compliant in good ones. They sing your praises to your face, but speak ill of you behind your back. "Another is a friend who becomes an enemy, and tells of the quarrel to your shame" (Sir. 6:9).

Finally, there are wastrel comrades who support you in unhelpful behavior. The Buddha said they will be your mate in drinking liquor and in roaming the streets at unseasonable hours. They will go with you to loaf at parties and share habits of gambling that lead to sloth. Some recovering alcoholics recognize this "friend" in the "drinking buddy" who helped them along the road into alcoholism.

True friendship. The Buddha also described qualities of true friends.[6] First, they help you. They watch over you when you are slack, guarding your property, protecting you in times of personal weakness. They are a refuge when you are afraid and supply you when in need. "A faithful friend is a sturdy shelter; those who find one find a treasure" (Sir. 6:14).

True friends remain unchanged when your fortunes change. "One who is a friend is always a friend and... is born for the time of stress" (Prov. 17:17). True friends tell you their secrets and also keep your secrets. They do not forsake you in trouble and will even sacrifice life for your good.

True friends tell you what is for your good. In this way, they keep you from wrong-doing and put you in the right way. By pointing out what you didn't know but need to know, they show you the right way to live. "One shows oneself a true friend who makes an honest reply" (Prov. 24:26).

True friends show affection for you. They rejoice in your good fortune and not when things go wrong for you. They defend you if others slander you and commend those who speak well of you. "Against your enemies [a true friend] will be your shield-bearer" (Sir. 37:5).

FRIENDSHIP AND SPIRITUAL PRACTICE

"As best you can...associate with the wise....Let all your conversation be about the law of the Lord. Have just persons for your table companions" (Sir. 9:14–16). Both the Buddhist and Christian traditions emphasize the role of true friendship in spiritual practice. We are to "encourage one another daily" (Heb. 3:13).

Buddhist perspectives. Ananda said to the Buddha that half of the holy life is friendship, companionship, and association with good people. The Buddha corrected him, saying that a good friend helps a person seriously live a spiritual life. So, "the whole of the holy life is friendship, companionship, and association with the good."[7] Buddhists call the spiritual teacher who helps you a *kalyana mitta,* a noble friend.

Sometimes we act against ourselves, mistakenly considering self-indulgence to be proper self-love. "Those who practice wrong conduct by body, speech, and thought do not love themselves. Even though they say, 'We love ourselves,' yet they do not....They do to themselves what a hater would do to someone....One who holds one's own self dear, with evil let that one not be linked."[8]

Because of this, a friend who sets us straight is a great gift in spiritual living. "Should you find someone who points out faults and who reproves you as if indicating a hidden treasure, follow such a wise and sagacious person. It is always better and never worse, to cultivate such an association. ...Such a one is dear to the pious and detestable to the worldly."[9]

Christian understandings. "If your brother [or sister] sins against you," Jesus taught, "go and point out the fault, just between the two of you. If they listen to you, you have won your brother [or sister] over" (Matt. 18:15). St. Paul echoes this: "If someone is detected in sin, you who live by the spirit should gently set that one right....Help carry one another's burdens" (Gal. 6:1–2). One who has a "truth-teller" friend is fortunate indeed! We can also reach out to share our difficulties with others. St. James exhorted us to confess our sins to each other that we may be forgiven (James 5:16).

By washing the feet of his disciples, Jesus modeled the kind of serving love he taught (John 13:14). St. Peter exhorted young Christian communities to this kind of friendship. "Above all, love each other constantly, because love covers over a multitude of sins. Offer hospitality to one another without complaining. Use your gifts to serve others....Anyone who serves should do it with the strength God provides" (1 Pet. 4:8–11).

IN CLOSING

Our preliminary reflections are complete. Part II teaches you how to do *brahmavihara* practice.

Part II

Doing the "Heavenly Abodes" Love Practices

Chapter 5

GETTING READY TO LOVE
Preparation for Loving-Kindness Practice

THIS CHAPTER explains how *metta* is practiced. It gives the blessings used in both informal and formal practice of *metta* and also describes the categories of beings and the spatial directions used in formal, intensive practice. The basic information in this chapter prepares you to understand the explicit instructions for doing the formal practice. They are given in the next chapter.

THE BLESSINGS

To practice *metta* we send blessings to various beings in a systematic way, beginning with ourselves. You may use any blessings you choose. Usually four or five is a helpful number. Customarily we go through all the wishes in order, sending them to the target person or persons, repeating them again and again during the time we practice *metta*. If you prefer, you may repeat each benediction more than once before moving on. However, be sure to keep repeating phrases; do not let your mind simply go empty.

Use the same blessings for everyone blessed during any one sitting of *metta*. If you are practicing formal, intensive *metta* to develop deep concentration, it helps to stay with the same phrases over the entire time of practice — for months or even longer. If you do *metta* informally for brief periods, you may choose different blessings for different sittings.

Here is a set of traditional blessings:

May I (you, all beings everywhere) be safe from inner and outer danger.

May I (you, all beings everywhere) be happy and peaceful in mind.

May I (you, all beings everywhere) be strong and healthy in body.

May I (you, all beings everywhere) tend my (your, their) life (lives) with happy ease.

These wishes, translations of very terse phrases in the Pali language in which the Buddha taught, have been used for many centuries. The first wish is that one be safe from *vera*,[1] which means hatred, revenge, or hostility. The threat or negativity may come from either inside or outside oneself. *Avera hontu* calls down upon people the wish that they live with peace, mildness, and non-hatred within and around them.

The second wish is that they be free of *byapajjha*, which means trouble, malevolence, an impediment or obstruction. This unwholesome root of ill will is a major mental impurity in Buddhist psychology. *Abyapajjha hontu* asks that people be free of wanting to do harm, free of mental impurity, that they have pleasant and positive states of mind.

The third word, *nigha*, means that which causes trembling. This refers to either physical or mental conditions, such as illness, rage, confusion, or fear. The word usually means concerns of physical health, though. *Anigha hontu* is a blessing for non-illness and undisturbed calm of body.

The final classical wish is *sukhi attanam pariharantu*. It means being able to manage life easily and happily, with few concerns or obstructions. One Buddhist teacher translates it "May they have ease of well-being."[2] This wish recognizes that taking care of ourselves is not always easy and that life can be consumed with many troublesome and time-consuming details. Meditation master Mahasi Sayadaw discussed this wish in terms of being able to bear the burden of our lives.[3]

Most Buddhist *metta* practice uses just these wishes, or a similar set of four. If you want to add a fifth wish, you may. It should be general enough that you can wish it for all beings. We have sometimes used "May I (you, all beings everywhere) come to union with God" in retreats.

BEFORE STARTING *METTA* PRACTICE

To do *metta,* we take a comfortable posture. You may sit, stand, walk, or lie down. Unless walking, closing your eyes usually helps. If you become uncomfortable, change your posture. You may start with a few intentionally deep breaths to relax. Some people like to focus attention at the heart.

Traditionally, we begin *metta* practice with forgiveness, which Jesus also said to do before spiritual practice. "If you are offering your gift at the altar and there remember that someone has something against you, leave your gift there in front of the altar. First go and be reconciled to each other; then come and offer your gift" (Matt. 5:23–24).

Practice forgiveness by saying something like this. "I ask forgiveness of all beings whom I have hurt or harmed in any way. I freely forgive all beings who have hurt or harmed me in any way. I freely forgive myself." We usually repeat this daily before practicing *metta.* This corresponds to the beatitude "Blessed are the merciful, for they will be shown mercy" (Matt. 5:7).

Before working with yourself, take a few minutes to recall some things about yourself that you can celebrate. We ponder helpful choices we have made to stir up feelings of gentle caring for ourselves. We need to know what is wrong with us, but that is only half the story. We need also to know what is right about ourselves. We must feel loving-kindness toward ourselves to feel it toward any other being. If you can think of nothing else, be pleased that you are learning to meditate.

When you work with any other individual in *metta* practice, it helps before beginning to take a minute to think of something positive about that person. Remember that the proximate cause for feeling *metta* toward others is seeing good in them. Looking for this good in others, however slight it might be, makes doing *metta* for them easier.

INFORMAL *METTA* PRACTICE

When practicing informally, always begin with yourself and end with "all beings everywhere." Use the same blessings throughout any given sitting of *metta*. However, at different sittings you may choose a different set of blessings. Start by offering each of your blessings for yourself. Go through the blessings in order; then start back at the top and keep going through them the whole time you are sending *metta* to yourself. Remember not to pause between phrases.

Those to whom you send *metta* in the middle may vary. You may move outward geographically — such as from yourself to all in the room with you, all in the city, the state, the country, the hemisphere, on earth. You may move out by emotional distance to benefactors (including parents), other family members, friends, colleagues, clients or students, acquaintances, people you don't know but see at times, and so on. When you work with groups of people, offer the wishes in the third person, for example, "May all beings in this city be safe from inner and outer danger."

To work with a problem relationship, go in order from yourself to a benefactor, then a friend, then a neutral person (someone you do not know well enough to have feelings about), and then the problem person. When working with a specific individual, address the wishes to that person in a "you" form, for example, "May you be free of inner and outer danger." Some people like to go through lists of friends and/or relatives in the middle part of *metta* practice. You can also send *metta* to animals, and some people bless their pets. Whenever working with an individual being, try either to image that being in your heart or in front of you, or else simply get a feeling of the being as personally present to you.

Doing occasional *metta* practice for short periods does not develop the same deep concentration and strong quality of *metta* that formal intensive practice does. However, the Buddha said that it is beneficial to do. "Developing your mind with *metta* for a brief period of time involved in milking a cow once in the morning, once in daytime and once at night time, or smelling a fragrance for once only, is far more advantageous than the offering of meals by cooking a hundred big pots of rice, once in the morning, once in the daytime and once at night time."[4]

Metta is a powerful practice of charity; not only does it send blessings to another, but also improves the quality of life for all beings by the changes it makes in the mind of the meditator. Even if you do not plan to practice *metta* formally, the remaining explanations in this and following chapters will still be helpful to you.

FORMAL *METTA* PRACTICE

The rest of the instructions assume that you have chosen to practice *metta* formally for some period of time. Be willing to work for months developing this skill, sitting every day or almost every day. It helps to sit at least half an hour or forty-five minutes a day when doing intensive *metta* practice.

This chapter next gives you the formal categories that are used and the directions to which *metta* is sent. The more specific instructions in the following chapter recommend how long to spend on each category. You may, of course, move more rapidly than we suggest. However, the more time spent on each category, the deeper the practice becomes. In retreats, people may spend two to eight or more months simply doing *metta* practice all day long.

In formal practice, the beings to whom we send *metta* fall into three categories. First are the personal categories, in which we direct loving-kindness toward particular individuals who play a role in our lives. Then come two sets of universal categories, in which we extend our gentle friendliness to all beings everywhere.

When you practice *metta* formally, you still begin with yourself. Once you finish each category, however, later sittings begin wherever you left off in all the groupings with which we work. Usually, you go back to earlier completed categories only if you run into a snag that doesn't resolve itself.

THE PERSONAL CATEGORIES TO WHOM *METTA* IS SENT

Formal *metta* practice begins with what are called the personal categories. These include:

- oneself,
- a benefactor (*piya puggala*),
- a friend,
- a neutral person,
- and what is traditionally called an "enemy."

We begin *metta* with ourselves because we are the being for whom we are most responsible. The Buddha also said, "Though in thought we range throughout the world, we'll nowhere find a thing more dear than self." This shocks some Westerners initially, as we are often taught we should put others before ourselves. This proper love of self, of course, does not mean self-indulgence or self-preference. A little reflection shows that the point is to have non-discriminating *metta*. If we discount ourselves, we will discount other beings. The Buddha goes on to say, "So, since others hold the self so dear, one who loves oneself should injure none."[5]

After working with ourselves, we go to the other personal categories. The texts say to choose living persons of the gender to which we are not sexually attracted.[6] In formal practice, we do not send *metta* to dead persons as we cannot reach states of deep absorption on a dead being. We also do not want to confuse our developing feelings of *metta* with sexual interest. Eventually you can offer *metta* to any living being, once the feeling is solidly established and you can recognize when it gets contaminated with foreign feelings.

After ourselves, we work with a benefactor. The benefactor should be someone toward whom you feel almost completely positive feelings. All human relationships have some ambivalence, but someone who has done us great good is likely to draw the least negativity.

The next object for *metta* is a friend. These relationships are usually not quite so purely positive as with benefactors. Thus we move here toward transcending some annoyances or even hostilities with our *metta*.

We then work with a neutral person — someone toward whom we have as little feeling of any kind as possible. It may be someone who rides your bus to work, but with whom you have never spoken. Or someone you see in the supermarket each week. Or someone who works in an office down the hall whom you occasionally see. We all have people in our lives whom we run into regularly, but with whom we have no relationship.

Finally comes the "enemy." We translate this term as "someone with whom you have trouble dealing." It is best not to start with someone who has grievously wronged you, but with someone you find only somewhat annoying.[7] As you work in this category, you can add other people and work your way toward more disturbed relationships.

If someone has seriously harmed you in the past, you may need to be fully in touch with all the feelings associated with the trauma before doing *metta* for that person. Sometimes counseling and support groups help. We often push uncomfortable feelings out of awareness, and *metta* ought not be used as a shortcut to avoid dealing with such feelings. Once the feelings are fully acknowledged and you want to be able to forgive, then you can more easily work with *metta* for the person.

THE UNSPECIFIED UNIVERSAL CATEGORIES

The unspecified universal pervasion of *metta* contains five categories that are all roughly synonyms for each other; each is a different way to say "all beings." By repeating the phrases over and over for each of these five categories, we emphasize by repetition that our *metta* is truly to extend to all beings. I translate these five categories as:

- all existent beings,
- all with breath of life,
- all distinct creatures,
- all individuals,
- and all embodied personalities.

The first Pali term is *satta,* from the abstract verb "to be." It thus literally means an existent being; however, it mostly refers to persons. In this context, though, it is one of the five ways to say "all sentient beings."

The second term, *pana,* literally means "a breather." It comes from the same stem as the Sanskrit word *prana,* which some readers will recognize as meaning the life energy. *Pana* generally means more than simply breath and has connotations referring to life energy.

The word *bhuta* comes from another root that means "to be." This word refers to what has being or has become. As the result of a particular becoming, it connotes the specific or distinct form that a given being takes. The next word, *puggala,* simply means a person or individual.

The final of these five categories has a more complicated derivation in the Pali language, being made up of two words. *Attabhava* means self-existence, one's own nature, form, appearance, or personality; it refers to the uniqueness of a given living form. The second word, *pariyapanna,* means gone completely into, gone into all that is meant by being in existence. *Pari* means around, and *appana* means endowed with what one has entered into. This word can mean embodied, and is so used in this context.

THE SPECIFIED UNIVERSAL CATEGORIES

The next seven — specified — categories are simpler, as they have easily understood meanings. My translation of the seven is:

- all females,
- all males,
- all who are saintly,
- all not yet saintly,
- all angels,
- all human beings,
- and all in states of suffering.

These seven categories fall into three distinct groupings. First is a gender division. We extend *metta* to all females and then to all males.

The next pair divides people into those who have reached at least the first enlightenment of the four posited in the tradition, and those who have not. Enlightened people are called *ariyas,* or noble ones. Since enlightenment implies saintliness, I have translated the term that way.

The Pali term *deva* literally means god; however, the gods referred to here are simply beings born in the higher realms in the Buddhist cosmology and are not very different from human beings. The closest Western term seems to be "angels," and that is the translation used here. "Human beings," *manussa* in Pali, is self-explanatory. The last category, *vinipatika* in the Pali, refers to all beings in realms lower than human. These realms are places of suffering, and their beings include hell realm beings; demons, who are like fallen angels; ghosts; and the many forms of animal existence.

THE DIRECTIONS

After working with the personal categories and these two groups of universal categories, we go to directional pervasion of *metta.* This simply goes through the twelve universal objects of *metta,* the five general and seven particular categories, doing each through all of ten directions.

The directions used are:

- eastern,
- western,
- northern,
- southern,
- southeasterly,
- northwesterly,
- northeasterly,
- southwesterly,
- downward,
- and upward.

These directions are considered to cover all possible locations of beings.

BEFORE STARTING *METTA* PRACTICE

The goal of intensive *metta* practice is a state called *simasambheda.* In this state, we no longer draw boundaries between ourselves and others. We do not discriminate between different types of persons, feeling good will for all equally. There is an examination on this attitude.[8] I will give it to you in the Postscript to this book. Please actually do intensive *metta* practice before challenging yourself with the exam. The next chapter gives detailed practice instructions.

Chapter 6

FILLING THE WORLD WITH LOVE
The Traditional Practice

IN TRADITIONAL PRACTICE, we work through the personal categories, the five unspecified universals, and then the seven specified universals. After work with the five and seven universal categories combined, we end with directional pervasion of loving-kindness to the twelve universal categories.

The amount of time suggested for each category is about how long it might take to be reasonably "finished" with it. Please stay with any being or category with which you are working well if it feels like there is still work to do. As long as it feels right, you cannot spend too long doing *metta* in any given category. Do not shorten the suggested time unless you feel quite certain that there is solid closure on that category, or you find it impossible to work with it at the time.

METTA TOWARD ONESELF

Begin with establishing posture and asking forgiveness as explained in the last chapter. Forgiveness is an important prelude to practice. "And when you stand praying, if you hold anything against anyone, forgive them, so that your Father in heaven may forgive you your sins" (Mark 11:25). Forgiveness makes us able both to give and to receive. Also, remember to recall some things about yourself in which you can rejoice. Then begin with these phrases, or similar ones of your own choosing. Remember to keep repeating the words; do not leave blank spaces between them. Try to focus on the meaning of the phrases as you say them.

> *May I be safe from inner and outer danger.*
> *May I be happy and peaceful in mind.*
> *May I be strong and healthy in body.*
> *May I tend my life with happy ease.*

In doing *metta,* it is not necessary to have warm feelings. Simply wanting to mean the phrases is enough, even when you feel like you might not *really* mean them. It is even enough to *want* to *want* to mean them. We cannot command feelings. Most people who practice *metta* have times with no feeling, but they testify that it still has effects so long as they practice as directed.

In a formal retreat, you work with yourself all day long for several days. If self-*metta* goes smoothly, you move to the benefactor after several days. If you cannot do *metta* for yourself, you can start with the benefactor. However, don't give up too quickly if there are difficulties. You can work with them. Remember that the Buddha said, "Who loves oneself will never harm another."[1]

If you cannot offer *metta* to your whole being, try extending it to some aspect of yourself you appreciate, such as the good you thought about before you started sending the phrases. Perhaps you can send *metta* to the aspect of yourself that wants to meditate or that values spiritual practice. If this works, practice it for a while, and then see if you can send *metta* to your entire being.

Do not worry if your mind wanders a lot while trying to practice, or if you feel sleepy or restless. These very common problems are discussed in chapter 11. Simply bring your mind back to the task whenever it strays. Do not be annoyed with yourself, and do not become impatient if progress in practice seems slow.

If you are sitting a half hour to forty-five minutes a day, try to work with yourself for about two weeks before moving on. This will give your practice a solid foundation.

THE OTHER PERSONAL CATEGORIES

Benefactor. When ready to move to the benefactor, choose the person you start with according to the criteria given in the last chapter. Think of the good this person has done for you to help awaken tender feelings. You may find it helpful to image the person — in your heart, in front of you, or some other way of your choosing. If you do not like imagery, or cannot easily do it, simply get a sense of the person as present to you in whatever way you can.

Then, as if speaking directly to your benefactor, offer the same blessings you called down upon yourself.

> *May you be safe from inner and outer danger.*
> *May you be happy and peaceful in mind.*
> *May you be strong and healthy in body.*
> *May you tend your life with happy ease.*

All the guidelines used for yourself apply, such as being sure to keep repeating the phrases and to focus on their meaning. Working with one benefactor for some time is very helpful, because it is about the easiest way to solidly establish *metta*. I suggest spending a month to six weeks on your benefactor.

If you run into negative feelings toward your benefactor, do not be alarmed. It is almost impossible for a human relationship to be entirely free of negativity. This practice helps purify our relationships by showing us where the glitches are. Simply acknowledge the feeling, and see if you can continue sending *metta*. It might help to recall again all that the benefactor has done for you. If the negative feeling gets too strong to continue *metta* for the benefactor, do a little *metta* for yourself, or some aspect of yourself, if that was successful.

Then when you are reestablished in *metta*, go back to your benefactor and try again.

If negativity is intense and long-lasting, focus your awareness on the negativity for a while. If you do insight practice, work with it that way. Be sure while acknowledging the negative feelings that you do not do anything to feed them; do not let yourself get lost in negative thought. If we simply let a negative feeling be, without encouraging it or trying to force it to leave, just looking at it, it often decides to lighten or leave.

If you get so bored with the one person that you really don't want to do the practice, try using a different benefactor. Don't keep changing benefactors, though; stay with any given benefactor as long as you can. If you simply cannot stay with this category for the suggested length of time, move on to the friend.

Friend. Select your friend according to the guidelines given in the last chapter. Do the suggested preliminary practices, including thinking of good things about your friend. Then begin to send the friend *metta* in the same way you did to the benefactor.

If you run into negative feelings, handle them as suggested for the benefactor. When sending *metta* to a friend, you can go back to the benefactor to renew the feelings of *metta*, if necessary.

Work with this category exactly as with the benefactor. I suggest spending a month to six weeks on it. After about a week, you can work with more than one friend.

Neutral person. The neutral person is the most astonishing category for many people. They are absolutely amazed to see that tender feelings can develop toward someone with whom they have no emotional interaction. These feelings often last for a long time after completing work with the person. The neutral person actually becomes very dear to us.

Guidelines for choosing the neutral person are given in the

last chapter. Work with this person as with benefactor and friend. You may not know enough about the person to think of good things about him or her. You can focus on the common human desire to be happy and realize that this person wants to be happy just as you do. If you run into negative feelings, which is less likely with this category, do *metta* for your friend until solidly reestablished in it. Work with a neutral person or persons for several weeks.

Enemy. It is recommended that you do not choose your most difficult relationships with which to begin work with the "enemy." Select someone who is slightly annoying to you. Work with them as with the above categories. If you run into difficulties sending *metta,* go to the neutral person, or to a friend or benefactor if necessary, to reestablish the *metta* intention.

You may work with several problem people while on this category, but stay with each one until the feeling of *metta* is solidly established. We want to be able to do as Jesus told Peter. "Then Peter came to Jesus and asked, 'Lord, how many times shall I forgive my brother when he sins against me? Up to seven times?' Jesus answered, 'I tell you, not seven times, but seventy-seven times'" (Matt. 18:21–22). However, remember not to move too quickly into very sensitive areas. Build your *metta* carefully. Choose the time you spend here according to how many people you need or want to work with. I suggest a minimum of two to four weeks.

THE UNIVERSAL CATEGORIES

Unspecified universal categories. After you finish the personal categories, work next with the five unspecified universal categories — those five synonymous phrases. Many people doing intensive *metta* find that working with these phrases brings a very deep and satisfying happiness. This probably is because of their sheer universality; each includes all beings without any exception.

With these categories, we do not directly address those to whom we are sending *metta,* as in the personal categories. You offer each of the four blessings for the first category, then go on to the second, third, fourth, and fifth — offering each all four wishes. Then you begin with the first again, and keep cycling through all five categories for the whole time you practice *metta.* You don't have to feel tenderness, but only to want to send *metta* to all without exception.

The phrases are:

May all existent beings be safe from inner and outer danger.
May all existent beings be happy and peaceful in mind.
May all existent beings be strong and healthy in body.
May all existent beings tend their lives with happy ease.
May all with breath of life be safe from inner and outer danger.... (through the remaining three wishes).
May all distinct creatures... (through all four wishes).
May all individuals... (through all four wishes).
May all embodied personalities...(through all four wishes).

Then begin again with "all existent beings." Remember to keep cycling through the four wishes for each of the five categories without pauses — a total of twenty blessings in each round. I recommend working with this grouping at least two to four weeks.

At some point, you may have difficulty saying the phrases. Do not worry about this. A shorter phrase may be easier to use; some alternative phrases are provided in Appendix IV. If all words become impossible, simply rest in the feeling of loving-kindness directed toward the beings you are blessing until the words return. Then keep repeating the words again. The reason the words sometimes go is explained in Part IV.

Specified universal categories. Next you work with the specified universal categories. We work with them as with the unspecified universal categories, going through all seven categories with the four wishes for each. The phrases are:

May all females be safe from inner and outer danger.
May all females be happy and peaceful in mind.
May all females be strong and healthy in body.
May all females tend their lives with happy ease.
May all males be safe from inner and outer danger...
    (through the remaining three wishes).
May all saintly ones... (through the four wishes).
May all who are not yet saintly... (through the four wishes).
May all angels... (though the four wishes).
May all human beings... (through the four wishes).
May all in states of suffering... (through the four wishes).

Then begin back at the start, and keep going through all seven categories with the four wishes each — a total of **twenty-eight** blessings in each round. I recommend two to three weeks on this.

Combined universal categories. Next we combine the five and the seven categories. We begin by offering the four wishes to "all existent beings," and then go right on without stopping through the remaining four unspecified categories and all of the seven specified categories, ending with "all in states of suffering." Then we start back at the beginning, and keep going through the four blessings for each of the twelve categories. Spend at least two weeks of daily practice on this grouping.

Each cycle here has a total of forty-eight blessings. As we add more length to one complete cycle with each area of the universal practice, keeping track of where we are demands increasing concentration. This practice strongly builds concentration, which is necessary for all forms of meditation you might practice.

THE DIRECTIONAL PERVASION OF *METTA*

The directional pervasion of *metta* can be done in two different ways. Choose whichever appeals to you. You may want to do it first one way, and then the other way.

The first method. First, go through all twelve universal categories; offer the four blessings for each category as you did with the combined category practice you just finished. Then go on with:

> *May all existent beings in the eastern direction be safe from inner and outer danger... (and continue with the remaining three blessings).*
> *May all with breath of life in the eastern direction... (offering the four blessings).*

Then offer in order the four blessings in the eastern direction for each of the remaining ten (three more unspecified and seven specified) categories. Then do all twelve categories, with the four wishes for each, in the western direction, then the northern direction, the southern direction, the southeastern direction, the northwestern direction, the northeastern direction, the southwestern direction, the downward direction, and the upward direction.

This makes a grand total of 528 blessings in each cycle! You will undoubtedly get lost more than once. When this happens, start where you think you most likely were. You will not be able to complete a cycle in one sitting unless you sit for quite long sittings. It may take you four or more sittings to get through the entire list once, depending on how long you sit for each sitting. When you resume sitting each time, just pick up where you left off at the end of the last sitting.

A second way. A second way to do directional practice with its 528 blessings takes one category at a time. It goes like this:

*May all existent beings be safe from inner and outer
danger... (and on through the remaining three
wishes).*

*May all existent beings in the eastern direction be safe
from inner and outer danger... (and on through the
remaining three wishes).*

*May all existent beings in the western direction...
(through the four wishes).*

Continue until you have given the four blessings to "all
existent beings" in each of the ten directions.

Then go to "all with breath of life," working as you did
with "all existent beings." Continue with the remaining ten
categories offering the four blessings for each, first without
specifying direction and then in each of the ten directions.

This practice is quite demanding on attention and very
strongly develops concentration. I recommend staying with it
at least a month before considering the directional pervasion
of *metta* completed.

THE NEXT STEP

When you finish the directional pervasion of *metta,* you have
completed basic training in *metta* practice. You can work
with any part of *metta* practice that appeals to you, or you
can deepen your *metta* practice by doing the whole series
again. If you would like to chant the practice you have just
learned, Appendix II offers a loose translation of a traditional
metta chant.

You have another option. The next chapter teaches you
how to do the other three *brahmavihara* practices: compassion, sympathetic joy, and equanimity. When we practice
intensive *metta* in retreats, we also do these other heavenly
attitudes after *metta.*

If you want to work with *metta* in a different way chapter 8 offers several methods for working just with human
beings, where we probably have our greatest need to develop

gentle kindness. Then chapter 9 gives suggestions for sending *metta* to beings in other realms. You might specifically want to work with animals, or perhaps with souls in purgatory.

If you feel that your practice experience has put you in a quite different space than ordinary waking consciousness, you are probably becoming quite concentrated. You can understand what is happening by learning how concentration develops in Part IV. This knowledge may encourage you to continue even more with your *brahmavihara* practice to attain deeper and deeper levels of concentration.

Chapter 7

ABODES OF THE GODS
Compassion, Gladness, and Equanimity Practices

BRAHMAVIHARA practice develops beautiful states of mind as it produces deeply absorbed concentration. The taste of the *brahmaviharas* can make you feel like you are already in heaven on earth. This bliss is far beyond the delights of grosser pleasures.

Brahma literally means noble, and *vihara* means dwelling place or abode. *Brahmavihara* is often translated "abode of the gods." Mahasi Sayadaw says that these states refer to noble living or "living in the exercise of good will."[1] They are called the "illimitables" because we develop them toward all living beings without exception; this gives them a potentially limitless range of influence.

Buddhist teachings also say that those who develop these states are reborn in the highest heavens in Buddhist cosmology — the *brahma* realms. Sixteen of these fine-material realms are open to beings who merit them. They have names like luster, aura, and great reward. These realms reward this practice differently, depending upon how deep is the absorption attained and how well-developed the practice is.

You have already learned how to practice *metta,* the first and foundational *brahmavihara.* In this chapter, you learn how to do the other three: *karuna,* compassion; *mudita,* gladness or sympathetic joy; and *upekkha,* equanimity. Traditionally, meditators formally practice these only after

completing the full *metta* practice given in chapter 6. It lays
the foundation for these further practices.

NATURE OF COMPASSION (*KARUNA*)

Compassion is a very important attribute in Buddhist
thought. It is one of the two "wings" of Buddhism, the other
being wisdom. *Brahmavihara* practice develops compassion,
as insight practice develops wisdom.[2]

The Buddha's compassion. After his enlightenment, the
Buddha realized that teaching people spiritual truths would
be an uphill battle. He felt disinclined to do it, until a *brahma*
being urged him to teach lest the world perish. The Buddha
reflected that there were some beings "with little dust in their
eyes"; that is, some people were ripe to do spiritual practice
if only shown the way. The Buddha resolved to teach out of
compassion.

Here are several lines from a second century hymn extol-
ing the Buddha's compassion:

> Without exception all this world was bound to un-
>   wholesome states.
> That you might free it you were long in bondage to
>   compassion.
> Which shall I praise first, you or the great compassion? ...
> Out of compassion for the world you have offered the
>   good *Dharma* for a long time."[3]

Some of the meanings of the very complex word *Dharma*
(*Dhamma,* in Pali) are the way, the Truth, the teachings,
Reality, the basis of all realities, that which upholds and sup-
ports us, and that by which we are led home. Similarities
to Christian understandings of both the Word and the Holy
Spirit are obvious.

The compassion of Jesus. Just as the Buddha taught out
of compassion, so did Jesus. He grieved when people would

not listen to what was good for them. "O Jerusalem, Jerusalem, you who kill the prophets and stone those sent to you, how often I have longed to gather your children together... but you were not willing" (Matt. 24:37).

Both Jesus and the Buddha also healed and worked miracles out of compassion. Jesus expressed such feelings when faced with a large hungry crowd. "I have compassion for these people.... If I send them home hungry, they will collapse on the way" (Mark 8:2–3). His compassion openly showed when he saw the grieving sister of dead Lazarus: "when Jesus saw her weeping... he was deeply moved in spirit and troubled.... Jesus wept" (John 11:33, 35).

When we develop compassion, we put ourselves in good company. We truly become a heavenly presence on earth. A bumper sticker reads: "Practice random kindness, and senseless acts of love." In a world torn by violence and hatred, what a beautifully compassionate stance this reflects!

Understanding compassion. Compassion is defined as the quivering of the heart in response to another's suffering. Compassionate beings want to eliminate the suffering of others when they encounter it.[4] They cannot bear to see suffering and remain unengaged. We need not always *do* something; not every instance of suffering calls for active involvement. Sometimes we act, sometimes just compassionately enter into the suffering.

Compassion is caused by seeing suffering in others. It directly combats cruelty and is successful when it ends cruelty. When we develop compassion to even a moderate degree, behaving cruelly or inflicting harm on any being becomes impossible.

Compassion is very different from pity or anger over suffering. With pity we condescend; we set ourselves apart from the suffering and "look down" on it. Anger dulls awareness of the sheer fact of suffering and makes it impossible to share it compassionately. Attempts to develop compassion have failed if our efforts produce sorrow, anger, or pity.

These states may mask as compassion, but are actually its dangerous "near" enemies.

Paradoxically, compassion has its own special quality of joy. It celebrates human bondedness, which gives it its delicate savor. As we acutely feel another's suffering, we share the happiness of human solidarity.

THE PRACTICE OF COMPASSION

Practice components.   Compassion practice uses the same categories of beings and the same directions as *metta* practice. However, we do not begin compassion practice with ourselves, but with someone who is suffering greatly. Since seeing suffering elicits compassion, it is most easily practiced where suffering is obvious.

Again, choose someone of the gender not sexually attractive to you. Avoid people to whom you are very close because you already have a mixture of feelings for them. If you believe some people deserve their suffering, they are also not the best first choice; it is easier to work with someone you consider worthy.

We use only one phrase for compassion practice. The classical phrase is something like: "May your suffering and sorrow come to an end" or "May you be free of pain and suffering." Some people are not comfortable with these phrases when they know the suffering will not end and prefer to use: "I care about your suffering." You also may use some similar phrase of your own choosing.

Doing compassion practice. To start compassion practice, hold an image of the suffering person, or have some sense of that person's presence. Begin to say the phrase you have chosen: "May your suffering and sorrow come to an end." Keep repeating the same phrase, over and over again. Work with your initial person for several weeks before moving to other beings.

Then go through the benefactor, friend, neutral person,

and enemy categories. All people have some suffering in their lives, so you can feel compassion for them even if not aware of specific suffering. Work with each of these categories as long as it feels appropriate. It will depend upon how many people you work with, and how clearly you get in touch with their suffering.

In doing compassion practice for particular individuals, you must get near enough to the suffering to feel it, but not so close as to get "lost" in it or be overwhelmed by it. If you stay too far away, you remain indifferent. If you get too close, you may fall into anger, grief, or pity. Be sensitive to your distance from the suffering, and adjust it as needed. If you have trouble feeling compassion for the benefactor, friend, or neutral person, go back to someone for whom you were able to feel compassion to renew the feeling, and then try again.

If you have trouble feeling compassion for the enemy category, reflect on the suffering their misbehavior has created for them. Both the Buddhist and Christian traditions teach that they will have a time of reckoning, that what evil they have done will have consequences. If you feel satisfaction because of their suffering, acknowledge this to yourself, and see if you can then do compassion practice. You can also renew the feeling of compassion with a category you did successfully.

After you complete the personal categories, work with both the unspecified and specified universal categories, as in *metta* practice. Use the "they" form: "May they be free of pain and suffering." Then do directional pervasion of compassion, in the *metta* format. Choose the length of time you spend on each category according to how deeply you want to develop compassion.

Some effects of compassion practice. As we can feel compassion for someone who has wronged us personally because of the self-suffering that person has created, so also we can feel compassion for those who cause havoc in the world at large. People who prey on others, who murder, steal, cheat, rape, or otherwise abuse others, not only inflict suffering on others but also on themselves. A measure of your compassion is how much you can feel it for such people.

People who are unhappy or anxious may be uncomfortable to be around, but they are in pain. People with unbridled desires, or consuming ambitions, are also suffering. Being caught in addictions or other bad habits is painful. Once compassion is developed, we easily see the suffering in the annoying habits or quirks of others. When these things draw compassion rather than irritation, the practice has done its work.

In some Buddhist traditions, meditators can take the "*bodhisattwa* vow." They vow not to enjoy liberation until they can bring all beings with them. Compassion makes them unable to go to their final reward in isolation and willing to continue in rounds of rebirth until all are saved.[5] Seeing our ultimate oneness makes individual salvation become meaningless to them.

NATURE OF SYMPATHETIC JOY (*MUDITA*)

Sympathetic joy, rejoicing in the good someone else has, is considered the hardest *brahmavihara;* human nature does not easily celebrate someone else's having something we may prefer to have for ourselves. I guarantee you that even the smallest taste of it is an extremely beautiful feeling.

Understanding sympathetic joy. The characteristic of sympathetic joy is gladness when seeing the success of others. The most important kind of success is spiritual, but sympathetic joy should not be limited to that. We become able to be happy for others on the terms in which they define happiness. We do not judge the source of their happiness.

Sympathetic joy directly combats envy. When developed we can see others' good without becoming envious; seeing their success causes gladness to arise. Sympathetic joy is successfully developed when it eliminates aversion toward others. Its near enemy, which looks like it but opposes it, is unfounded merriment, getting caught up in frivolous excitement.

Advantages of practicing sympathetic joy. The word *mudita* means rejoicing and getting pleased. Sometimes it is translated as gladness. When others' success is truly pleasing to us, we are delighted frequently — whenever we hear of or see another's happiness. When I was doing intensive *mudita* practice, this reflection came to me: the sun never sets in one place, but it rises in another; if we are happy for those who have sunshine, our own lives will never lack it.

Since we will cherish others' good as if it were our own, we will feel caring and protective of them. In this way, aversion toward others is first diminished and then vanquished. When others' good makes us happy, resentment and envy have no place.

PRACTICE OF SYMPATHETIC JOY

Categories of practice. *Mudita* is practiced with the same categories as compassion and *metta*. The only difference is with whom we start. Choose someone toward whom you have positive feelings who is enjoying happiness or success. Even a very small delight or pleasure will do. One commentary says to choose someone whom thinking about makes your heart smile. If you don't know of any happiness in the life of someone you appreciate, choose someone who makes you or others smile by their presence. You can celebrate this joy.

Again, use only one phrase, something like "May your happiness and success never end," or "May you continue to enjoy happiness and success." The phrase in Pali more literally translates as asking that another not be deprived of whatever wealth has come that person's way. True wealth means more than money or material possessions.

Practicing sympathetic joy. First, direct sympathetic joy toward the happy person you chose. Once the feeling gets reasonably well developed, go through the benefactor, friend, neutral person, and enemy categories. If you run into difficulty, return to a former category that worked well. Remember, though, that the intention is the important thing. Not actually feeling happiness for another is no problem, as long as you are not in negative feelings such as envy or resentment. Wanting to offer the blessing is the important factor.

After the personal categories, do both sets of universal categories, as with the earlier practices. Then do directional pervasion of sympathetic joy.

NATURE OF EQUANIMITY (*UPEKKHA*)

Equanimity is by far the hardest *brahmavihara* for Westerners to understand. It rests on the Buddhist understanding of *karma* (*kamma,* in Pali). It asks us to remain unmoved by the outcomes, or lack of outcomes, of our former *brahmavihara* practice. It asks us to accept without a negative reaction whatever happens in our own and others' lives.

Understanding equanimity. Technically, equanimity is one form of what Buddhists call neutrality of mind. The Pali word literally means "there in the middleness." This attitude of impartiality and balance prevents bias or preference. When directed toward human beings it becomes the *brahmavihara* of equanimity. It looks on all beings, and what happens to them, without any prejudices or preferences, free of all discrimination.

However, equanimity is not indifference, which is its near enemy. Were it indifference, we could not feel *metta, karuna,* and *mudita.* Equanimity does not mean failing to act when action is called for, or accepting all manner of evils without doing anything about them. We act when action is called for.

Equanimity leads us to act out of wholesome motives rather than in unskillful reaction to events.

Understanding *karma*. We cannot exhaustively consider *karma* here, but a few words seem helpful. The Buddha outlined several laws of cause and effect. The Western world recognizes three types of those laws — those governing physical matter, biological forms, and mental phenomena. The Buddha also delineated a law of moral cause and effect, the law of *karma*.

Most people have erroneous, simplistic understandings of *karma*, believing it means "an eye for an eye, a tooth for a tooth." It is really about the consequences of choices; every choice we make bends the mind just a little bit in one direction or the other. *Every choice* — there is no "just this once won't count!" Over time, we shape our minds into certain kinds of character, and this determines our outcomes in the future.

This is very like Christian understandings of judgment and of the effects of sin. In both traditions, the bottom line is that we have some choice in what happens to us, we are responsible for our choices, and choices have consequences.

Values of practicing equanimity. Equanimity prevents excesses and keeps loving-kindness, compassion, and sympathetic joy in proper bounds. It also helps us understand that whatever we might wish for another being, we cannot control their outcomes. These are determined by their actions, according to the choices they make. Equanimity keeps our lives and relationships in balance. When we are balanced, we do not try forcefully to make the world, other people, or their lives conform to our wishes.

PRACTICE OF EQUANIMITY

Categories for equanimity practice. Equanimity practice uses the same format of practice as the other *brahmav-*

iharas. Practice begins with a neutral person, someone in whom we have no personal investment. If your former work with neutral persons developed tenderness toward them, choose a new one for this practice.

One statement is used. "Your outcomes depend upon your actions and not my wishes" is a good one. Some people prefer, "Things are just as they are." You might like "I leave you in the hands of God." Use a phrase that reflects the wisdom of knowing that you cannot control what will happen for other people.

Doing equanimity practice. Begin with your neutral person, repeating the same phrase over and again. When unbiased acceptance has developed, move to the other personal categories of benefactor, friend, and enemy. If you run into problem feelings, go back for a short time to a category where you had success, and then return to the one giving you difficulty.

After you finish the personal categories, do the universal ones, and then the directional pervasion of equanimity, as with the other practices. When you finish this, your basic training in *brahmavihara* practice is complete.

WHAT COMES NEXT

The next two chapters offer some specialized ways to work with *brahmavihara* practice. Some people will prefer the traditional practice, while others may find these suggestions help keep practice fresh and new.

Part III

Alternative Forms of "Heavenly Abodes" Practice

Chapter 8

OVERCOMING HATRED
WITH LOVE

Loving-Kindness toward Human Beings

HUMAN BIRTH is considered rare in Buddhist thought with its rich, multi-layered cosmology. "To gain birth as human is hard indeed...and it is hard to hear true spiritual teaching."[1] The rare occurrence of having both human birth and access to spiritual teaching is to be greatly treasured, for the human is the easiest realm in which to mount a spiritual practice.

The Christian tradition similarly values highly the worth of each individual. Each is seen as a creation of God, called to return to God. In spite of the many reasons we have for treasuring the well-being of each other, we often do not do so.

This chapter looks at several alternative ways to practice *metta*. They are directed only toward human beings. There is some loss in not sending *metta* to all sentient beings without distinction. However, such practice is suggested because we greatly need to treat each other more kindly. In the next chapter, practice for other beings, including animals, will be offered.

A UNIVERSAL CATEGORIES PRACTICE

Our first format for sending *metta* just to humans parallels the classical Buddhist one for unspecified and specified universals. Its unspecified universal categories are simply synonyms for human being. The specified universals include the list of beings that the Buddha named in the *Metta Sutta* with gender, from the traditional practice, added to it. The Buddha, of course, applied this list to all beings, but it can easily be applied only to people for this purpose.

Unspecified universal categories. This format uses the following unspecified categories:

- human beings,
- individuals,
- members of the human family,
- people,
- and persons.

To practice, simply take each of these five groups through the four wishes as you did with the groups of traditional practice. It looks like this:

> *May all human beings be safe from inner and outer danger.*
> *May all human beings be happy and peaceful in mind.*
> *May all human beings be strong and healthy in body.*
> *May all human beings tend their lives with happy ease.*
> *May all individuals...(through each of the four wishes).*

Then take, in turn, "all members of the human race," "all people," and "all persons" through the four blessings. To work with just this grouping, simply run through these five categories over and again for the duration of your sitting period.

Specified universal categories. Here we need more than the seven categories of the traditional Buddhist practice if we use all that the Buddha put into the *Metta Sutta* and, as seems appropriate, both genders. We have these categories:

- female people,
- male people,
- frail people,
- strong people,
- tall people,
- stout people,
- medium-sized people,
- short people,
- thin people,
- heavy people,
- people we have met,
- people we have never seen,
- people living far away,
- people living nearby,
- people already born,
- and people waiting to be born.

To practice these categories, go through the list offering each of the four blessings for each category in turn. This group can be practiced apart from the unspecified universals, and also in combination with them, as is done in the traditional practice.

A PRACTICE TO REMOVE PREJUDICES

The next of these alternative practices is for healing racial and ethnic prejudices. The world's various ethnic groups are broken into eight clusters, which cover most existing human diversity. Seven of the eight groups are found in any medium-sized city in the United States. We work with people in these groups across different ages. It is also helpful to distinguish by gender for each category. The groupings selected and the format for practice with them follow.

Ethnicities. The ethnic groups with which we work are, in alphabetical order, people of:

- African descent,
- East Asian descent,
- European descent,
- Latin American descent,
- Mid-Eastern descent,
- Native American descent,
- South Pacific descent,
- and mixed racial descent.

Most of these groups are self-explanatory. The Mid-Eastern group is made up of dark-skinned Caucasians of Asia and North Africa; their appearance often differs considerably from lighter skinned European Caucasians. The Native American group includes both American Indians and the Innuit of the north polar region. Only the very dark people of the South Pacific, including Australian aboriginal people, are not regularly found in most of our American communities.

These groups are listed in simple alphabetical order, putting the racially mixed group at the end. If you have strong prejudices, you might want to order the groups with your most preferred group first, working your way down to your least preferred group. That way you would offer *metta* first to those for whom it will be easiest. If you do not like the way the world's ethnic groups are divided up, you can create your own ethnic categories to do essentially the same practice. The only caution is that you should make it universal, being sure you tried to cover all the ethnicities represented in the world.

Ages. In my own experimental work with the *metta* practice, I found working with age groups very helpful. For the types of people who were least appealing to me, starting work with a very young and vulnerable age made the *metta* start to flow much more easily. After some age-group work, I recalled that in the *Metta Sutta* the Buddha included those waiting to be born as objects of *metta*, so I added them. This yielded the following age groupings:

- the unborn,
- infants,
- young children,
- teenaged children,
- young adults (20–35),
- middle-aged adults (35–50),
- mature-aged adults (50–65),
- elderly adults (65–80),
- and very old adults (80+).

One practice format. For one way to practice, start with the very youngest age, divided by gender, going through the different ethnic groups. Then move up to the next age, and follow the same procedure. Here is how it looks:

May all unborn girls be safe from inner and outer danger.
May all unborn girls be happy and peaceful in mind.
May all unborn girls be strong and healthy in body.
May all unborn girls tend their lives with happy ease.
May all unborn girls of African descent be safe from inner and outer danger.
May all unborn girls of African descent... (through the remaining three wishes).
May all unborn girls of East Asian descent... (through the four wishes).

Then go through all the other ethnic groupings. Next do the same practice with "all unborn boys."

Then go through the four blessings for "all baby girls," first without ethnic specification and then through all the ethnic groupings. Next do "all baby boys" in the same manner. Then, in succession, do "all young girls," "all young boys," "all teenaged girls," "all teenaged boys," "all young women," "all young men," "all mid-aged women," all mid-aged men," "all mature-aged women," "all mature-aged men," "all elderly women," "all elderly men," "all very old women," and "all very old men."

Each of the gender/age groups is first done through the four blessings without ethnic specification, and then taken through these blessings for each of the ethnic groupings. Your practice will end with: "May all very old men of mixed racial descent... " (through all four wishes).

A second practice format. The above practice can be done differently by taking each ethnic group by itself through all the ages. For example:

> *May all females of African descent be safe from inner and outer danger.*
> *May all females of African descent be happy and peaceful in mind.*
> *May all females of African descent be strong and healthy in body.*
> *May all females of African descent tend their lives with happy ease.*
> *May all unborn girls of African descent... (through the four blessings).*
> *May all baby girls of African descent... (through the four blessings).*

Continue on through all the ages with the four wishes, specifying females of African descent at each age. Then do for males of African descent as you did for females. Then work your way through each of the other ethnic categories in the same fashion.

You may want to try the practice in both these formats. In whichever form you practice, be sensitive to your reactions to each group you specify. You might find your reactions to gender, age, or ethnicity differences the same across the board. However, you may be surprised at how some of the gender/ethnicity/age categories affect you. You may react strongly in either positive or negative ways to one category, while a neighboring category draws a different reaction.

Do not be dismayed by any prejudices you uncover, but simply work with the *metta* practice as best you can. It will bring healing if you are faithful to it, and you will be surprised to see how it can radically change previously negative attitudes.

A PRACTICE TO DEVELOP
WORLDWIDE CONCERN

Another alternative practice with humans develops global consciousness. It brings feelings of bonding and tenderness toward people living in various areas of the world regardless of their other characteristics. For this practice, we use the same age and gender distinctions, but work with spatial directions, or areas of the globe, rather than with ethnic groupings.

Spatial directions. The spatial directions used here eliminate the downward and upward direction done in classical Buddhist practice; many people find it difficult to think of human beings in such a context. In place of them, the directions start with one's own community and country. The directional categories used are:

- this community,
- this country,
- eastern direction,

- western direction,
- northern direction,
- southern direction,
- to the southeast,
- to the northwest,
- to the northeast,
- and to the southwest.

One practice format. One way to practice this form is to start with the most tender age, as we did above with ethnicities. We work up to people of very old age, across genders, and in all the directional categories. This practice looks like this:

May all unborn girls be safe from inner and outer danger.
May all unborn girls be happy and peaceful in mind.
May all unborn girls be strong and healthy in body.
May all unborn girls tend their lives with happy ease.
May all unborn girls in this community be safe from inner and outer danger.
May all unborn girls in this community... (through the remaining three blessings).
May all unborn girls in this country... (through the four blessings).

Then take "all unborn girls" through the remaining directions, eastern through southwestern, with the four wishes. Next do the same practice with "all unborn boys."

Then go through the four blessings for "all baby girls," first without directional specification, and then through all the directions. Next do "all baby boys" in the same manner. Then, in succession, do "all young girls," "all young boys," "all teenaged girls," "all teenaged boys," "all young women," "all young men," "all mid-aged women," "all mid-aged men," "all mature-aged women," "all mature-aged men," "all elderly women," "all elderly men," "all very old women," and "all very old men."

Each of the gender/age groups is first done across the four wishes without directional specification. Then it is taken through the four blessings for each of the ten directions from "in this community" through "in the southwestern direction." Your practice will end with: "May all very old men in the southwestern direction..." (through the four wishes).

Another practice format. As we did with ethnicities, so we can do with directions, taking our blessings, by gender, through all the ages for each direction. It goes like this:

> *May all females in this community be safe from inner and outer danger.*
> *May all females in this community be happy and peaceful in mind.*
> *May all females in this community be strong and healthy in body.*
> *May all females in this community tend their lives with happy ease.*
> *May all unborn girls in this community... (through the four blessings).*
> *May all baby girls in this community... (through the four blessings).*

Continue on through all the ages, with the four wishes, specifying females "in this community." Then do the same for males "in this community" as you did for females. Then work through each of the other directions in the same fashion.

You may find your mind dwelling on the suffering in particular areas of the globe as you do this practice. This is not a problem, for that can serve as a basis for your *metta*. The practice will actually increase your sensitivity to the issues that human beings all around the globe confront regularly. It fosters an attitude of seeing the world as a global community.

CREATIVE COMBINATIONS

Simple age, ethnicity, and direction practice. Develop your own creative combinations to keep *metta* practice fresh and new. You might work with the age, ethnicity, or direction categories as you did with universal categories, not breaking them down further. For example:

> *May all people of African descent... (through the four wishes).*
>
> *May all people of East Asian descent... (through the four wishes).*

Then simply continue through all the ethnic groups with the four blessings, and keep going through this list over and over again for your *metta* sitting.

You can do similarly with age or direction categories. You also can go through two or all three of these lists, one after each other, and then keep starting back again at the beginning of this longer list throughout your sitting. You may want to do one or more of these lists with gender specification.

Crossing *Metta Sutta* categories with other categories. You might take the categories from the *Metta Sutta* and work with them across age, ethnicity, or direction. For example:

> *May all frail people in this community... (through all four blessings).*
>
> *May all frail people in this country... (through the four blessings).*

Take "all frail people" through the remaining eight directions with all four blessings. Then go on with:

> *May all strong people in this community... (through all four blessings).*

After you take "all strong people" through all the directions with the blessings, then continue through all the types of beings in this list across all the directions with the blessings. This form of practice ends with "all people waiting to be born in the southwestern direction." You could similarly take the *Metta Sutta* list across age or ethnicity categories.

IN CLOSING

There are many possible combinations in the various groups of categories given you. Freely create whatever formats or new categories are meaningful and helpful to you. You might want to work with various religious or political beliefs, for instance. For those who like to chant, a *metta* chant for human beings is presented in Appendix V.

There are no rules preventing you from sending *metta* to any group that you wish. All the formats for practicing *metta* can also be used to practice any of the other *brahmaviharas*, too. When working with groups of people, *brahmavihara* practice is most helpfully done when you do not single out only a particular favored group. If you create your own categories, try to form companion groups that truly have a universal scope.

We now move on to other beings. The next chapter teaches a special practice for animals and beings in other realms.

Chapter 9

BLESSING ALL BEINGS

Loving-Kindness for Animals and Beings in Other Realms

METTA is to be extended to all beings without exception. While it seems most crucial that human beings deal with each other more kindly, other beings also need considerate treatment. People differ in their sensitivity to the suffering of animals and in their ability to realize that animals, too, do not want to be hurt, killed, or feel terror. People also differ in their beliefs about the possibility that beings exist in other realms, such as heaven or hell. In the Buddhist tradition, human beings are encouraged to send blessings of loving-kindness to all beings in many different realms of existence.

SENDING *METTA* TO ANIMALS

The first precept in Buddhist morality is not to kill any form of sentient life.[1] This is not limited only to those animals we love to touch or pet. It also includes the kinds that crunch if we step on them, that whir or buzz around our heads, and that instill fear in us. Practicing *metta* for animals extends this non-harming attitude into one of positive well-wishing.

Effects of *metta* toward animals. At Insight Meditation Society in Barre, Massachusetts, where I frequently do long meditation retreats, animals seem to sense the non-harming atmosphere. Birds regularly alight on people's outstretched hands, even when they are not holding food. Chipmunks may come up to you, rise up on their haunches, and appear to be begging for something. (I give them peanuts.) Dogs flock to the place from miles around; meditators must be asked to ignore them, so that they will be willing to return to their proper homes. Sometimes dragonflies "ride" on you when you are doing walking practice outdoors.

Those who feel tenderness for animals will probably most be drawn to practicing *metta* for them and will find that it supports their loving attitude. The practice could be even more beneficial for those who consider animals "things" to be used for their own sport and pleasure. It would be hard to do *metta* regularly for any beings without its making our attitudes toward them more benevolent. For those interested in extending *metta* to these creatures who share our planet with us, we offer some suggestions for practice.

Some animal categories for *metta*. For one form of practice with them, animals are divided into six size categories:

- huge animals,
- large animals,
- medium-sized animals,
- small animals,
- tiny animals,
- and minute animals.

Huge animals refer to such creatures as whales and elephants. Large animals include horses, cows, and tigers. Medium-sized animals are those such as cats, dogs, and goats. Small animals include rats, fish, birds, squirrels — and my friends, the chipmunks. Tiny animals are most insects, worms, butterflies, and like-sized creatures. Minute animals are microscopic or nearly so.

The following practice also breaks animals into groups depending on the surface of the earth in or on which they move. This list includes animals that move:

- underground,
- on land,
- in water,
- and in air.

Finally, major zoological types of animals are delineated:

- simple spineless animals,
- worms and snail-like animals,
- insects and spiders,
- fish,
- amphibians,
- reptiles,
- birds,
- and mammals.

This list is based on a general zoological classification of animals. Microscopic animals are lumped together with sponges and jellyfish in the first category. The second category also combines several classes of animals. Insects and spiders are both called arthropods. Amphibians, such as frogs and salamanders, move both on land and in water. Reptiles include animals like snakes, turtles, and crocodiles.

The form of practice. Here is how this practice looks:

> *May all huge animals be safe from inner and outer danger.*
> *May all huge animals be happy and peaceful in mind.*
> *May all huge animals be strong and healthy in body.*
> *May all huge animals tend their lives with happy ease.*
> *May all large animals be safe from inner and outer danger.*

*May all large animals... (through the remaining three
wishes).*
*May all medium-sized animals... (through the four
wishes).*
May all small animals... (through the four wishes).
May all tiny animals... (through the four wishes).
May all minute animals... (through the four wishes).
*May all animals that move underground... (through the
four wishes).*
*May all animals that move on land... (through the four
wishes).*
*May all animals that move in water... (through the four
wishes).*
*May all animals that move in air... (through the four
wishes).*
*May all simple spineless animals... (through the four
wishes).*
*May all worms and snail-like animals... (through the
four wishes).*
May all insects and spiders... (through the four wishes).
May all fish... (through the four wishes).
May all amphibians... (through the four wishes).
May all birds... (through the four wishes).
May all mammals... (through the four wishes).

You can go through all these categories one after the other
as we have listed them. You also could choose to work with
just one of the three separate sublists, taking only size, space
moved in, or zoological classification. There are no rules
about what categories to use; do what feels most comfortable for you. Whatever categories you work with, take the
four blessings through them over and again in a sitting.

Directional pervasion of *metta* to animals. You can
add directional pervasion of *metta* to animals. Take any one
of these three lists, or all of them together, through the classi-

cal directions (in chapter 6) or the ones suggested for human beings (in chapter 8). For example:

May all huge animals ... (through the four wishes).
May all huge animals in the eastern direction ...
(through the four wishes).

Then take "all huge animals" through the four wishes for each of the remaining directions. Then send the four wishes to all animals of each of the other sizes in each of the ten directions, if doing the size classification. You may choose just that, or just the space moved in or zoological classification, or all three together.

Metta to animals in different habitats. Any or all of the three lists of animals can also be taken through a listing of possible animal habitats. Here is such a list:

- bogs, marshes, and swamps,
- cities,
- deserts,
- farmland,
- forests and woods,
- glaciers and ice packs,
- heath and tundra,
- jungles,
- lakes and ponds,
- meadows,
- mountains,
- oceans and seas,
- plains,
- rivers and streams,
- valleys and vales.

Practice crossing these habitats with the biological classification list looks like this:

May all simple spineless animals in bogs, marshes, and swamps be safe from inner and outer danger... (and through the remaining three wishes).

May all simple spineless animals in cities be safe from inner and outer danger... (and through the remaining three wishes).

"All simple spineless animals" are then taken through each of the habitats in the list with four wishes for each habitat. Then do likewise for "all worms and snail-like animals," "all insects and spiders," "all fish," "all amphibians," "all birds," and "all mammals."

An alternative practice with habitat. These habitats need not be crossed with any of the first three categories given. This list can be used by itself, sending the four *metta* wishes to "all animals" in each of these types of places. This would simply be:

May all animals in bogs, marshes, and swamps be safe from inner and outer danger... (and on through the remaining three wishes).

May all animals in cities... (through the four wishes).

You continue through the list of habitats with four wishes for "all animals" in each of the habitats.

These suggestions should help you make whatever combinations will increase gentle kindness toward animals in your own heart. Of course, you can also create many other possible categories of your own choosing. In addition to *metta*, we can also send the other *brahmavihara* blessings to animals. A *brahmavihara* chant for animals is given in Appendix VI.

SENDING *METTA* TO OTHER REALMS

In formal practice, we do not send *metta* to specific beings who have died from human life; the form in which we knew them no longer exists. We do not know in what form they may now be existing; this makes it difficult to get the proper sense of them to send them *metta*. It is also taught that we cannot get deeply concentrated sending *metta* to the dead. For these particular beings, though, we may share merit, which is an act of loving-kindness.

Sharing merit. Meritorious actions are said to make us "shine within." We create merit with various virtuous acts, such as piety and goodness; spiritual practice is said to create powerful merit. We can share merit with any other being, whether living or dead. Sharing merit is itself a meritorious action and increases our own merit. So the more we give away to others, the richer in merit we become. This is not considered the best motive for sharing merit, however!

To share merit, use a simple formula like this. "May the fruits of my (generosity, virtue, spiritual practice) be for the good of (my mother, "John Doe," all beings everywhere)." Name the meritorious action and the being(s) with whom you wish to share. You can also go through a list of meritorious acts, repeating the phrase for each of them, naming a different meritorious action each time. The merit for successive virtuous acts can be shared with the same or different beings.

Beings in other realms. Although in formal practice we cannot send *metta* to specific dead human beings, we can send *metta* to the beings in other realms as a group. Buddhist cosmology is rich in realms, but you need not accept this framework to send *metta* to other beings.

Buddhist cosmology lists a large number of hell realms created by hatred and various animals realms created by delusion. The realm of hungry ghosts is created by greed, and that of demons is created by self-centeredness. These realms are lower than the human one; they are places of suffering.

Above the human realm are six *deva* realms, realms of lesser gods. One gets to a *deva* realm by practicing generosity and virtue to a high degree. Above the *deva* realms are a great variety of *brahma,* or high god, realms. One gets there by exceptional mental purity, attained through the development of very high levels of concentration. *Metta* and other *brahmavihara* practices develop the kind of mind that merits a *brahma* realm.

Buddhists see all these realms as temporary way-stations. They all fall short of the goal of Buddhist practice, which is *nibbana,* the only reality not subject to conditions. They can all be seen as places of purgatory. Buddhist rebirth is said to occur when one is not yet sufficiently pure for *nibbana* and must continue to experience conditioned reality until completely pure. Buddhists, of course, also see human life as a place of purgation.

Parallels to Christian perspectives. Buddhist teachings about these realms have many similarities to Christian belief. Many Christians *do* believe in hell and also believe that there are fallen angels. The demons in Buddhist thought are described very like the Christian notion of fallen angels.

The way the *devas* and *brahmas* are described makes them sound like the various hierarchies of angels in Christian thought. The word *deva* means bright or shining. *Deva* beings are seen as quite like humans; their bodies are described much like the way the risen body of Jesus appeared.[2] *Brahma* bodies are considered to be much finer, unable to be seen by humans, and the highest *brahmas* do not have bodies, but only minds.

Teachings about rebirth are a lot like the Christian teachings on purgatory. Pope Gregory the Great held the opinion that each person's purgatory will be at the places on earth where that person had committed sin.[3] Many Christian mystics have described human life as a purgatory. The idea behind purgatory — wherever it may be or take place — and rebirth is the same; only completely pure beings can go to their final end, so we must continue to have opportunities to be purified until purification is complete.

Universality of belief in angels. Even in materialistic America, a surprising number of people believe in angels; a 1988 Gallup poll found 50 percent of adult Americans endorsed this belief. Since then, many publications on angels suggest that interest has increased.[4]

An informal survey by *Time* magazine in late 1993 found 69 percent of Americans endorsed belief in angels.[5] Forty-six percent of these people believe they have a personal guardian angel, and 32 percent say they have experienced angels. There is also strong belief in devils, or fallen angels, with 49 percent of people expressing belief in these beings. Most believers (55 percent) hold that angels are a special kind of being, rather than just ghosts of the dead or creations of imagination.

Jews, Christians, and Muslims call them angels. Hindus and Buddhists call them *devas*. They are guardian spirits for Native Americans, and *fravashis* for the Zoroastrians. Whatever they are called, these beings all hold many characteristics in common. They are frequently quite interested in human beings and can and will be helpful to those they choose to help. They bring messages, announce and explain God's actions, help prevent disasters, care for people in need, and guide those willing to listen. Some groups, notably Mormons and Muslims, believe that angels brought God's major revelations to humans.

Sending *metta* to beings in other realms. You may send *metta,* or any other *brahmavihara* blessing, to all beings in any other realm — to beings in hell, to angels, or simply to beings in purgatory without specifying a place of that purgatory. Choose the realm to which you wish to send *metta,* and offer the four blessings to all beings there.

You may prefer to put together a list of different levels of the other realms — such as the angels, archangels, principalities, authorities (virtues), dominions, powers, thrones, cherubim, and seraphim given us by Pseudo-Dionysius.[6] The highest angels, cherubim and seraphim, are said to exist just to worship God. Thrones bring justice, while dominions regulate life in heaven. Virtues work miracles, and powers protect human beings from evil. Principalities care for the welfare of nations. Angels and archangels are special messengers and guides to individual people. These functions mirror some ascribed to *devas* or *brahmas* in Buddhist thought.

Your *brahmavihara* list could also include beings in hell for different kinds of wrongdoing, similar to the levels of hell that Dante sketched in his poetic voyage there.[7] Buddhist hells also manifest different degrees of suffering, and different wrongdoings call for sojourn in different hells. *Metta* can be offered to all beings at the levels both higher and lower than human. Practice would cycle through all these categories over and over again as in other formats already presented.

For those specially interested in praying for the souls in purgatory, *metta* offers a new and beautiful way of doing that. Sending *metta* can be an especially potent way to do good for beings in the purgatorial process. A *metta* chant for beings in other realms is offered in Appendix VII; it incorporates both Christian and Buddhist perspectives on purgation.

IN CLOSING

This chapter completes all instruction in how to meditate. In the next part, we explain types of meditation and problems you might encounter. We also describe the course of development in meditation forms like *brahmavihara* practice.

Part IV

Concentrative Meditation: Problems and Development

Chapter 10

WAYS TO TASTE HEAVEN
Understanding Concentrative Meditation

MEDITATION PRACTICES can be categorized in different ways. Christians have long distinguished between discursive meditation, which involves reflective thought, and what is called contemplation. The Buddhist tradition works chiefly with two very broad types of non-discursive meditation: concentrative practice and uncovering, or insight, practice. We will look at both these classifications and also at how *metta* practice fits into these understandings. We then will outline some benefits of concentrative meditation. This chapter will not explore insight practice, since the book's focus is a concentrative practice.

TWO BROAD WAYS
OF CLASSIFYING MEDITATION

Discursive meditation and contemplation. For most of Christian history, beginners in spiritual life have been told to do discursive meditation. It consists of working with the cognitive faculties to image and think. The rationale is that we must start where we are, using these natural abilities. Unfortunately, some spiritual guides are afraid to let people do anything but such practice.

For the mystics, discursive practice was only the beginning.[1] Mystical treatises recognized that such prayer becomes burdensome at some point, or the mind simply refuses to work in the normal way. When concentration is well developed, it can no longer sustain thought. Knowledgeable guides tell meditators to quit trying to do discursive meditation when this happens.

When discursive practice can no longer be sustained, meditators are considered to be in contemplation. Contemplation is seen as a gift from God that happens to us more than being something that we do. We can dispose ourselves but cannot make contemplation occur. In this non-discursive state, we are actively receptive and remain "held" to the object of meditation.

Concentrative and uncovering meditation. For Eastern traditions, meditation is *not* thinking, and they hold that we must stop thinking to meditate deeply. They do allow limited amounts of reflection at the start of meditation practice.

What do they *do,* since they also know that we cannot produce captivated attention by an act of volition? In concentrative practice, attention is held on *one* particular object — a word, a phrase, a sensory experience, an image.[2] The object differs in different traditions and sometimes in different phases of practice. You try to close out everything else, going deeper and deeper into being with just that one object. Whenever your mind wanders, you let go of the wandering as soon as you become aware you have strayed and go back to the meditation object.

A second kind of meditation is awareness, or insight, meditation. The movement is almost exactly the opposite from concentrative meditation. In insight meditation we try to become aware of as much of what is going on as we can, so we will have many different objects of focus. This is not just letting your mind wander, though, for very disciplined methods guide how we do this. So, in concentrative meditation, we have one object; in awareness, or insight, meditation, there are many. We do not discuss insight meditation in depth in this book.[3]

THREE FORMS
OF CONCENTRATIVE MEDITATION

We now look in more detail at discursive practice as a concentrative technique. Then we consider two methods of non-discursive concentrative practice: "watching" the object of meditation in one location, and in more than one location.

Discursive practice as concentration. Concentration can develop to some degree using "thinking" or discursive techniques. The quite limited concentration attained reaches only the lower levels of absorption.[4] One common Christian method of discursive practice is using reading, commonly scripture, as a "starter." Another is doing the *Spiritual Exercises* of St. Ignatius of Loyola.

The practice called *lectio divina* starts with reading, goes to reflection, then to prayer, and finally into contemplation. When something in the reading captivates our attention, we ponder it. When it ceases to hold us, we move on to another passage. Ideally, we become absorbed enough in one passage to move into spontaneous prayer and then deep stillness with it.

The Ignatian *Spiritual Exercises* are a detailed examination of the human condition and the life of Christ. The meditator works with imagery, reflection, and prayer; two major formats of practice exist. One is a month-long retreat, spending most of the day working with the *Exercises*. In the second, you work over many months, outside of retreat, spending some time each day on it.

Another way to do discursive practice focuses attention on some notion or idea, holding the mind to pondering just that notion. We might reflect, for example, on love or Jesus or peace.

Buddhists use many objects for reflective practice. One set includes such recollections as the qualities of the Buddha, the Buddhist teachings, the Buddhist community, morality, generosity, *devas,* death, the characteristics of *nibbana,* and the parts of the body.[5]

Less appealing to Westerners is reflection on ten different stages in the decomposing of a corpse. Although we are not likely to choose this as a meditative object, I have found that during long retreats of Buddhist practice, it sometimes simply starts happening. While walking during one retreat, I saw a dead cat by the roadside. I was drawn there, day after day, to see what happened, until finally someone removed it. It had gotten to where worms were crawling in and out of body orifices. Reflection on such objects can bring us to the lower stages of concentration.

Some objects of meditation that might start as discursive reflection can become more deeply concentrated practice. This happens in *brahmavihara* practice, which you are learning in this book. The first three *brahmaviharas* — *metta,* compassion, and sympathetic joy — can bring us to a very high state of absorption, with only one stage remaining in work with a tangible meditation object. The fourth *brahmavihara,* equanimity, takes us to that last stage.[6]

Meditation with one object at one location. We now turn to non-discursive concentrative meditation. One practice is watching *one* object at *one* location. This method brings the most deeply penetrating concentration of all. It is also very hard to do unless you have already developed some concentrative capacity. The classic example is using a *mantra* or sacred word and holding it in a particular place in mind or body. A Christian Eastern Orthodox example is holding the name of Jesus in your heart. Hindu yogis may hold the name of Rama or Krishna in the heart. Some use a *mantra* that contains the vibrations of a divine attribute and hold it at some point of concentrated spiritual energy.

We also can use an external object to develop concentration, if that is easier, like a candle flame or geometric figure. We must be careful not to use an object that encourages thinking. If you put the name of Jesus in your heart, you must *not* start thinking about Jesus. Since many people would tend to think, the Benedictine monk John Main, who studied meditation techniques with an Indian teacher, suggested using the Aramaic word *Maranatha*, which means "Come, Lord Jesus." A word in another language is less likely to lead to thought. Hindu *mantras* usually are not actual words, but are just syllable sounds related to different aspects of deity.

Other inner objects can be used as the meditative focus of concentration. You may visualize a flame in the heart, a symbol of divine indwelling or of the Holy Spirit. Some image a diamond between the eyebrows, symbolizing divine wisdom. Sometimes we concentrate on light or sound somewhere in the body. All of these have particular spiritual benefits catalogued by the traditions that use them. They also greatly calm autonomic nervous system activity, which brings health benefits.

The Theravadan Buddhist tradition, from which your *brahmavihara* practice comes, uses watching the breath in insight practice, its other major meditation practice. We watch it at one location in the body — nostrils, chest, or diaphragm — to build the concentration needed. When doing insight practice, we repeatedly return to the breath to keep ourselves sufficiently concentrated.

Concentrative practice is said to slowly transform your being into the attributes of the deity or virtue on which you concentrate. Of course, we speak in terms of years of practice here. A classical story illustrates the transformation such practice seeks. A novice meditator told his teacher that he had trouble holding his mind on the meditation object because he kept thinking of his pet ox. Each day when the teacher came to his hut to get a report, it was the same story. Finally, the teacher told the student, "Just concentrate on your pet then." One day soon thereafter, when the teacher called the student out of the hut to report, he said he could not come out because his horns were too big to get through the doorway. Delighted, the teacher realized the novice had achieved strong concentration and told him to return to his original meditation object.

Meditation on one object at different locations.
A second kind of non-discursive concentrative meditation, watching one object at different places, is somewhat easier to do initially. The classic example is watching the breath flow in and up the nostrils, into the chest, down into the diaphragm, and then back out. Sometimes we carry a *mantra* or sacred word on the breath when doing this. Breath in itself has many spiritual connotations in the different traditions — such as the Holy Spirit in Christianity. Watching breath move is easier than concentrating in one location. The restless mind is given some activity; we give it a track on which to run.

In some spiritual traditions, such practice has quite specific purposes. A common one is to open communication between different parts of the being. For example, we might move a *mantra* back and forth between the eyebrow and the heart centers of energy. Or we might move a *mantra* or some other symbol up and down the spine to awaken the *kundalini,* or spiritual energy.

This method is a very common part of the training of shamans or witch doctors in some preliterate spiritual traditions. Many different subtle points in the human body are seen as gateways to different realms of existence and different planes of being. One takes consciousness to these planes by becoming adept at using these body points as an exit. So shamans, who sometimes go after the departing soul of a dying person to bring it back, learn how to go to and return from these realms safely. They visit various demonic and heavenly planes.

Such training is generally restricted to those who have a calling to this vocation for the good of their community. Needless to say, it should *not* be practiced heedlessly, as it is full of dangers. Unfortunately, some peddlers are now on the road inviting people to try shamanism. One can only hope that they know little beyond preliminary practices, such as concentration on different rhythms or drum beats, so that they will not precipitate vulnerable people into catastrophe.

It is entirely safe to watch your breath flow in its natural path. You can also image a flow between forehead and heart, or other points at least as high as the heart. Definitely do *not* work with body points below the heart, as they contain very powerful energies that you might not be prepared to manage. *Any* experimentation with moving different symbols or images along any body pathways lower than the heart or out of the body should be done only under the guidance of a competent spiritual teacher.

In Hindu yoga, these advanced practices come after years of working with a *mantra* or other concentration object. They can bring up experiences that may overwhelm an unprepared person. Spiritual practice is *not* without *very* real dangers — most of which can be prevented by proper work with a qualified teacher. Unfortunately many Westerners treat these profound practices as if they were parlor games.

METTA MEDITATION AND CONCENTRATION

Now we very briefly sketch development of *brahmavihara* practice. This practice can bring you to all the necessary stages of concentration. The next two chapters flesh out this broad overview with more specific information on both problems and development in practice.

At the beginning. Unless you have worked extensively with concentration, your mind will wander a lot. This expectable experience is nothing to be alarmed about. Also, if you have not practiced meditation before, the body will likely complain about sitting still for some time. You may also have bouts of sleepiness, restlessness, boredom, and reluctance to do the practice. All these problems are discussed in the next chapter.

In early stages of *brahmavihara* practice, we often consciously think about the blessings we are sending. This is not a problem, as it helps keep us on target initially. Thought should be confined to the blessings and the person blessed, however. We do not want to let the mind wander aimlessly.

The beginning of ease. At some point, which may not come the first time you go through the course of *metta* practice, the practice becomes easier. You must still make the effort to put your mind on practice, but it may feel like something "automatic" starts to happen. The mind is more willing to do as you tell it, and you are more willing to make the effort.

You find that you easily rest in the meaning of the phrases, almost like seeing behind the words. At times the wishes flow with extraordinary ease. You are no longer bothered with restlessness and sleepiness. Consequently, there is less reluctance to practice; often practice feels so satisfying that you are eager to do it.

A time of bliss and excitement. Still later, practice becomes both exciting and blissful. The wishes may seem like they no longer flow, but simply "float" full-blown in your mind. You may find a shorter phrase works better, and at times words just disappear. Stay with the *metta* feeling if this happens.

Intense waves of pleasure may delight the body, and enthusiasm pervade the mind. Sometimes involuntary movement occurs, and it also can feel like you are floating. You might feel like you are bursting with good will toward everyone.

Sometimes people become overly enthusiastic and decide that they must be quite holy for such experiences to happen. A knowledgeable guide is helpful at this time to keep you on track with practice, to assure you that your experiences are well-known phenomena, and to disabuse you of egoistic self-inflation.

The deep quiet. Although delightful, the previous time was just a stage in practice, and not the highest. As the practice really starts to deepen, very intense quietude and stillness develop. The happiness is so subtle that it must be experienced to be really understood. Practice becomes very simple, with the feeling that almost nothing is happening.

The meditation object may just simply "hang," full and complete. Words may be impossible. We just keep sending out the feeling of *metta*, on which we are intensely, unshakably focused.

SOME BENEFITS OF MEDITATION

Although meditation is primarily a spiritual practice, it brings many other benefits. Medicine and psychology have documented them.[7]

Health benefits. Some of meditation's fringe benefits are physical: lower blood pressure, lower resting pulse rate, relaxation, release of tension, even occasional medical healing. There are also emotional benefits: calming emotional arousal and stress, clarifying emotions, and getting in touch with emotions before they start to move us around. Mental benefits include better concentration; freedom from mental wandering that keeps us chewed up inside; freedom from fretting, stewing, and worrying; and developing the ability to focus and stay focused. With consistent work, there also comes greater ability to control impulses that get us in trouble — and even to see the kind of states of mind that lead to our problem behavior.

Occasionally, people report adverse effects from various forms of meditation. The difficulty most often comes from inability to relax, fear of loss of control, or improper method. Consultation with a competent teacher should help.

The main benefit. The therapeutic benefits of meditation are all by-products and not the main goal of practice. Meditation is, in its heart and core, a spiritual practice. We must embed it in a life reflecting a broader spiritual perspective and discipline. This is needed to reach the fullest flowering of our meditation practice, so it can give us all that it has to give.

The goal of spiritual practice is God, and all the other therapeutic effects are simply "fringe benefits" that occur along the way. However, those who want less can and do meditate for various therapeutic benefits, and they *do* get them.

Chapter 11

NOT TO BE INTIMIDATED!
Common Problems in Meditation

THIS CHAPTER discusses problems of both beginners and more advanced meditators. It is based on Buddhist understandings and illustrated with comments from St. Teresa of Avila. She cautioned: "It is very important in the initial stages of prayer not to be intimidated by thoughts."[1] We must not let any of the common problems in meditation practice intimidate us.

BEGINNERS' PROBLEMS

Two experiences are very common at the beginning of meditation. Unless we cope with them, they can derail our practice.

Discomfort. First is discomfort. Moving disrupts meditative concentration, and our bodies are usually not accustomed to sitting still. Ordinarily as soon as small tensions start to build in the body, we move without even knowing it to relieve the distress. When we try to sit still to meditate, body tension can start to build.

This is a problem only if we let it be. We must discipline the body to sit still, but we also ought not brutalize ourselves. Patient, gentle persistence is the answer. When discomfort becomes more distracting than movement, then we move or scratch or do what is needed to relieve the problem — and then start again. Over time, the body will settle down.

Wandering mind. The second common beginner's problem is wandering mind. This is so pervasive and so common that it seems almost funny to call this universal experience a problem. It usually takes years of practice before we can tell the mind to stay put and actually have it obey. Yet we must keep trying, for if we just sit and daydream or wool-gather, we are no longer meditating.

To develop concentration, holding onto the concentration object is very important. You must keep the *metta* phrases going, keep saying your sacred word, or keep renewing an image you are working with. Whatever your "tool" of practice is, do not let go of it too soon. And it will be too soon, if you can still repeat it or be with it.

St. Teresa was adamant about this:.

> Taking it upon oneself to stop and suspend thought is what I mean should not be done;...because...we would be left like cold simpletons and be doing neither one thing nor the other. When the Lord suspends the intellect and causes it to stop, He Himself gives it that which holds its attention.... Thinking you can make [the soul's faculties] be quiet is foolish.... This effort to suspend the intellect is not very humble. Although there may be no fault, there is no lack of a penalty; labor will be wasted, and the soul will be left with some little frustration.... It has used its energy and finds that it hasn't achieved what it wanted to achieve with it.[2]

Using your sacred word or *metta* phrases does not guarantee good concentration. Your mind will still wander. But it will wander a lot less, and concentration will continue to develop, if you keep working with the tool. Some people who practice Christian concentrative meditation let go of their object as soon as they start to feel grounded or centered. This is a serious mistake. In the beginning stages of practice, it invites wandering mind to take over. Other problems are also associated with it.

Unconscious eruptions. Another danger is that contents of the unconscious mind can surge into awareness prematurely. They may be more than the meditator can handle. Ordinarily, in concentrative practice, such experiences emerge only in advanced stages when equanimity is highly developed enough that we have the ability simply to accept them.

A major reason for such emergence is prematurely abandoning the tool. Some meditators enjoy letting go of their tool, simply sitting in emptiness. This creates a void in the mind, and all sorts of content can rush in. Teresa of Avila said that people who so empty their minds think they are enjoying a high state of prayer, but she was certain that this is a mistake. She called it "foolishness" and said that their religious superiors should cut their prayer time way back and give them useful duties to do.[3] Voluntarily trying to make the mind blank is not helpful.

Other problems. Some people have a lot of sleepiness early in practice. Our minds are not accustomed to being both still and alert. Usually one of two things happens. Either the mind says, "Nothing's going on so it's time to go to sleep," and you feel overpowered by drowsiness. Or else the mind says, "Nothing's going on; it's time to stir up some excitement." Then you get very restless. Wandering mind gets worse, and the body may even become agitated. Buddhists have deeply studied these problems that hinder meditation practice.

THE HINDRANCES

The Buddhist tradition has identified five special problems that cause great difficulty in our practice until we have solidly developed concentration.[4] We must deal with these hindrances vigorously to keep practice from derailment.

Greed. The first hindrance, greed, covers several of the Christian capital sins, especially avarice, lust, and gluttony.

This attitude clings to what is pleasant or appealing. When we get lost in long trains of thought, greed is at work. We are amazingly attached to our thoughts and often do not want to relinquish them to meditate. However, we must willingly empty out such mental activity to meditate.

Other forms of greed intrude. Sometimes we spend meditation time trying to keep a particular feeling happening. When we have a pleasant meditation experience, we want to sink into it, get lost in it. Foggy, unclear absorption feels very good, but we are no longer meditating when we lose sharp clarity of mind.

Sometimes we want to wallow in emotions — even unpleasant ones like guilt or sadness, as well as delightful ones like lust. We may enjoy dramatizing ourselves in self-pity or self-blame. We may even justify wallowing in so-called spiritual emotions, like guilt, by claiming that it is good to encourage such feelings. However it shows itself, indulged greed is a potent hindrance to spiritual practice. We must simply say "no" to ourselves and refocus attention on our meditation object. If we are committed to practice, this can be done.

Aversion. The second great hindrance is aversion. Just as greed wants to hold onto something, aversion wants to push something away. It covers the capital sins of anger and envy. It also covers emotions like fear, guilt, sadness, and resentment.

St. John of the Cross says that fears are "usually very great in spiritual persons who have not reached [the] state of spiritual marriage."[5] Fear can potently affect spiritual practice. We are afraid of physical or emotional pain and pull back. We are afraid to really throw ourselves into the practice because of what we might experience. St. Teresa said, "There are many who begin, yet they never reach the end. I believe this is due mainly to a failure to embrace the cross from the beginning."[6]

Teresa also says we must persevere through hard times

when "there is nothing but dryness, distaste, vapidness, and very little desire.... [The serious meditator] is determined, even though this dryness may last for [one's] whole life."[7] "The love of God does not consist in ... delight and tenderness, which for the greater part we desire and find consolation in; but ... in serving with justice and fortitude of soul and in humility."[8]

When things we do not want to experience happen, anger or sadness often follows. We may get annoyed with everything in the environment — anything we can find to blame. Or we become dejected and want to give up. Sometimes we get mixtures of all these feelings. We must acknowledge them and realize that such situations do not create anger, sadness, or fear. They show us the tendencies our hearts are harboring. Reminding yourself why you are practicing can help get you back on track.

Sloth/Torpor. The third hindrance, sloth and torpor, obviously corresponds to the capital sin of sloth. Sleepiness and boredom are the major ways this hindrance is manifested.

Sleep is an excellent escape from a tedious situation and can destroy practice if we let it. Buddhists have a long list of antidotes to sleepiness. These include sitting with open but unfocused eyes, looking at light, washing face and eyes with cold water, pulling the earlobes up and down until they are hot, and practicing standing up.

Boredom comes from lax attention. We can best handle it by bringing attention closer to the meditation object and meticulously holding it there.

Anxiety/Restlessness. The fourth hindrance is anxiety and restlessness — either of body or mind. It can be manifest as obsessive thinking. One common form is guilty ruminating, replaying memories of past mistakes over and again in the mind, and feeling bad about ourselves. When guilt is about past actions that we have acknowledged and abandoned, we ought simply to acknowledge the feeling, not feed it by thinking about it, and turn back to our meditation practice. If we feel guilty about bad conduct we have stopped doing, but haven't admitted to anyone, confession often helps. If it is over bad behavior not yet given up, we need to make very firm resolutions about the behavior.

We may also obsess over plans for the future or worry about other people. It helps to remember that obsessing does not accomplish anything positive and that your thought about your baby or anyone else is *not* that person. Obsessive thinking and body restlessness can be ways we avoid meditating.

Doubt. The fifth and most deadly hindrance is doubt, which can completely close practice down. Doubt takes several forms; we can doubt the practice, the teacher, our own ability or suitability for practice, or the time or place for doing practice, among other things. Usually decreased effort comes before doubt. Redoubled effort is the antidote; having a commitment we are determined to keep helps make this possible.

Doubt is a tricky issue. Obviously we do not continue to invest in every option we explore. However, you do not give a practice sufficient opportunity to show what it can do for you unless you make some investment. Often we start doubting as an excuse to stop meditating when we do not want to do it. To keep doubt from closing down practice, making an agreement with oneself about commitment helps. If we have firmly agreed with ourselves that we will practice for a certain length of time, when doubt occurs we simply remind ourselves.

Faith. Now a few comments on faith as the Buddhist tradition sees it. My first experience with such an understanding came in my twenties when I simply could not feel certain about what I thought I ought to believe as a good Catholic. After several false tries, I finally found a knowledgeable priest who helped me see the difference between faith and conceptual beliefs. He told me that faith was not feeling certain about ideas, but wanting God strongly enough to "risk" your entire life in seeking God.

At first, this terrified me; I wanted the security of certainty. Now it seems the only reasonable way to look at faith. Faith cannot mean coercing our minds to think in certain patterns of thought or to hold ideas that are not really grounded in our experience. That would be clinging to opinions, a serious mistake according to Buddhist thought.

The Buddha encouraged people to try out in their own lives any practice or teaching that appealed to them. We taste a practice; we find out what its fruits are. Experience then either confirms or disconfirms its value for us. We never affirm teachings that we have not tried. We simply acknowledge that we do not know them experientially.

INTERMEDIATE PRACTICE PROBLEMS

Sinking mind. Once concentration starts to develop, new problems emerge. "Sinking mind" means getting lost in a foggy, amorphous, blissful state of deep concentration, but with very little clarity. Because this feels so good and people enjoy it very much, many are little inclined to let go of it. Sometimes people spend years "blissing out" like this when they think they are meditating. However, the lack of clarity signals to most that all is not exactly well. Meditation requires keeping high clarity in deep concentration.

The major difficulty with sinking mind is unwillingness to relinquish it. With willingness, there are techniques to help. The most important is again the tool one uses — sacred word or *metta* phrases, for example. When concentration gets strong enough to "bliss out," many people don't like using the tool because it seems to put some distance between them and the delight. Repetition of our tool helps keep attention bright and alert. If we stop because sinking into bliss feels so good, we easily fall into fogginess.

The author of *The Cloud of Unknowing* said that "empty"

prayer is "by invitation only."[9] And remember the counsel of St. Teresa.

> When God desires to suspend all the faculties...the soul is occupied completely in loving the One whom the intellect labored to know, and loves what it didn't understand, and rejoices in so great a joy that it couldn't have experienced it save by losing itself in order...to gain itself....There is a small lack of humility in wanting to raise the soul up before the Lord raises it....This little speck of lack of humility...does much harm to progress in contemplation.[10]

Attachment to delight. However delightful this middle period of practice is, snags appear. Most people become quite attached to its delights. They tend to interpret experiences in ways flattering to vanity and self-importance.

This period of blissful ease lasts for differing lengths of time — most typically for years. It is a terminal point in some people's practice; for some reason further progress simply does not occur. This period cannot end until we willingly cease clinging to meditative delight.

GENERAL PROBLEMS

Psychic inflation.   Psychic inflation afflicts almost all people once they have some experience beyond ordinary waking awareness. In other words, a person appropriates these experiences, considering them a "possession" of his or her ego. We might need a competent spiritual teacher to deflate this egotism. If left to be, it becomes a potent hindrance to further spiritual work. Some people even believe themselves to be enlightened, or in a very high state of prayer, when they are little beyond rank beginners.

Improper technique. Other people wrongly apply techniques they have been taught, or else develop their own techniques that include mistakes that could be avoided by working with a method that has proven itself over time. Usually, an inadequate technique only wastes time, but sometimes people accidentally open up experiences for which they are not prepared. The premature eruption of unconscious contents that we already discussed is one such problem. Faulty technique occasionally produces symptoms of imbalance in either body or mind. Serious disturbances are rare, but some individuals so stress their nervous systems that they feel effects for a long time.

Mourning loss. For a long time into spiritual practice, positive experiences are fleeting. However, they can be quite intense and fill us with desire for more of them. Once we taste spiritual realities, we feel a real sense of loss when they go — and they *will* frequently leave us. We must accept that we will feel such loss keenly, without letting it swamp us or derail us.

Self-deception. For some meditators, experiential knowledge of God comes. They may feel touched by their personal deity in ways they cannot deny. Anyone believing they have such experience needs to work with a competent guide, as there are obvious dangers of self-deception. St. John of the Cross urges immediately turning one's mind from such experiences since the grace God means to bestow occurs in the minute of its coming. We do not add anything helpful by obsessing about such experiences, and may fall into vanity and self-preference.[11]

Chapter 12

WATERING THE GARDEN
How Concentration Develops

MEDITATION PRACTICE goes through clearly defined stages. Although each person's experience is unique, some common features define each stage. The course is somewhat different for concentrative and insight practices, although there are many similarities. This chapter limits discussion to concentrative practice. We first look at the mental factors that occur in states of concentrated absorption, and then at different levels of absorption. Our theoretical framework is mainly Buddhist.

St. Teresa of Avila deeply understood these stages. For the first four, she used the metaphor of watering a garden:

> The garden can be watered in four ways. You may draw water from a well (which is for us a lot of work). Or you may get it by means of a water wheel and aqueducts...by turning the crank of the water wheel.... The method involves less work than the other.... Or it may flow from a river or a stream.... The ground is more fully soaked, and there is no need to water so frequently. ...Or the water may be provided by a great deal of rain.... and this way is incomparably better than all the others mentioned.[1]

We illustrate the stages primarily with Teresa's work, since she described them so clearly.

FACTORS OF ABSORPTION

Both the Hindu and Buddhist[2] traditions have lucidly explained the factors of mind that define concentrative absorption. These factors are also found in other traditions' descriptions of concentration, although their psychology of them is not so developed.

Initial application. Initial application is directing the mind to the object of concentration. In early meditation practice, we must do this continually, over and over again, because the mind keeps slipping off. We must deal with wandering mind, discussed in the last chapter, until concentration becomes established.

At some point the task becomes easier. We still make the effort of aiming the mind at the concentration object, but it stays more willingly at the task. The absorption factor of initial application has ripened. It is like clearing away handfuls of earth so a spring can run. You must continue getting the earth out of the way, but it becomes easy once you settle into the task and no longer rebel against it. Initial application occurs in the first level of absorption, but drops off as we become more concentrated.

Sustained application. Once we put the mind on the object of concentration, we must keep it there. This is sustained application. In our spring analogy, once you have cleared away all the obstructing earth, you may have to hold back debris from the sides of the spring to keep the water running.

Another analogy is like polishing silver. Initial application is like putting the rag with silver polish on the silver; sustained application is like continuously rubbing the silver. This factor also drops off in higher levels of absorption.

Zest or rapture. While we must *do* initial and sustained application, we cannot make zest, which is also called rapture, happen. It is caused by maintaining an intense, concentrated, and interested focus on the meditation object. This most striking factor of absorption can produce startling experiences.

It can make you feel like you are levitating, and trustworthy people claim that it can actually make this happen. St. Teresa of Avila reported: "It was impossible for me to resist, but it carried off my soul...without my being able to hold back — and sometimes the whole body until it was raised from the ground."[3] The most intense rapture often comes after initial and sustained application have dropped off. But it, too, leaves before the two highest levels of absorption.

Delight or happiness. Delight is a subtler experience than zest. Most people experience it as a very delicate sense of total well-being. The body feels light and effortless, and the mind is clear and alert. When delight is strong, people can sit for long hours in meditation without feeling any discomfort. This factor leaves before the highest level of absorption.

One-pointedness. One-pointedness is simply the mind's staying stably on its object. It is the "real stuff" of concentration, defining it. This factor stays through all the levels of absorption; without it, there is no concentration.

Balance or equanimity. Some balance is present from the first stage of concentrative absorption, but it blossoms in the last stage. It replaces happy delight and leaves us able to accept all experience with neither positive nor negative feelings.

FIRST STAGE OF CONCENTRATION

The first five factors listed above define the first stage of concentrative absorption.[4] When absorption starts, meditation practice ceases to be so much work and takes on an "automatic" quality. Most people can tell that consciousness has changed, although initially they usually cannot explain what happened.

When you enter this state, the five hindrances discussed in the last chapter end. These are primarily problems in getting absorbed. In absorption, there is no greed for other experiences, no aversion, no sleepiness or boredom or dullness, no restlessness or anxiety, and no doubt about what you are doing. St. Teresa said, "The soul that begins to walk along this path of mental prayer with determination and that can succeed in paying little attention to whether this delight and tenderness is lacking...has traveled a great part of the way."[5]

Thought can remain in this first stage of concentration, but it stays focused on the meditation object. From St. Teresa: "This discursive work with the intellect is what is meant by fetching water from the well."[6] Initially, we go in and out of this stage frequently. You can be in the first absorption briefly, then wander, and then go back into it — over and again.

SECOND STAGE OF CONCENTRATION

This stage begins when initial application drops off.[7] The mind is so stable on the object that it stays "put" without continually renewing application. Sometimes the first and this second stage collapse into one. Since sustained application also ends after this stage, this means that both initial and sustained application leave together for some people.

Subtler experience. The mind's "flow" to the meditation object becomes much subtler in the second stage of absorption. St. Teresa said: "All this that takes place here brings with it the greatest consolation and with so little labor that prayer does not tire one, even though it lasts for a long while."[8] The *brahmavihara* blessings simply flow by themselves.

The mind more rests in their meaning than it thinks the

phrases. St. Teresa also wrote of this subtler penetration of the object: "It has happened to me that while in this quietude, and understanding hardly anything of the Latin prayers,...I have not only understood how to render the Latin verse in the vernacular but have gone beyond to rejoicing in the meaning of the verse."[9]

Hallucinatory experiences.   Some people experience subtle lights and sounds, often beginning about this stage. Some forms of practice draw this out more than others. Even early in meditation practice, people may have some hallucinatory experiences — that is, seeing when there is no visual stimulus, hearing when there is no auditory stimulus, and so on.

Many situations can cause sensory experiences in the absence of stimulation. Sometimes illness will cause them. St. Teresa apparently suffered from tinnitus, as she complained of a cacophony of noise in her head — all sorts of whistles and tweets and bird sounds.[10] Since most people associate hallucinations with mental and emotional disorders, some meditators worry if it happens to them. However, it is no cause for alarm. We hallucinate when we dream, and meditation is just another experience that draws it forth. Mentally disordered people usually believe such experiences come from something outside themselves, while experienced meditators can recognize that they are meditation-induced.

Auditory experience in meditation often begins with the sound of surf or swishing. We can also hear bells and chimes ringing loudly, very subtle "high frequency" sounds, and even human voices. Visual experiences can be of lights, colors, geometrical symbols, faces, scenes, and so on. Some people feel touched or pulled, and some smell various odors and taste unusual tastes.

The body can feel greatly distorted. Body parts may feel like they are in the wrong location on the body. Sometimes particular parts feel ballooned out or grossly large, while others feel flattened or squashed. Deep concentration is the major cause of such experienced distortions. Regardless of which senses are involved, St. John of the Cross repeatedly urged meditators to place no importance on such experiences.[11]

THIRD STAGE OF CONCENTRATION

In the third stage, both initial and sustained application have ceased,[12] and zest often dominates experience. One-pointedness is very strong. "The faculties have only the ability to be occupied completely with God. It doesn't seem that any one of them dares to move, nor can we make them stir unless we strain to distract ourselves."[13] Words may stop coming for periods of time; using a shorter *metta* phrase is sometimes easier.

Intense pleasure. We feel deep touches of bliss, peace, happiness, and serene tranquility. Typically so much ease, joy, and delight tempt almost everyone into believing that surely they have completely arrived, and that there can be nothing beyond this. Buddhists call this time "pseudo-nirvana" for that reason.

St. Teresa vividly described it: "This prayer is a glorious foolishness, a heavenly madness where the true wisdom is learned; and it is for the soul a most delightful way of enjoying."[14] "The joy is so great that it sometimes seems the soul is at the very point of going forth from the body."[15] We quickly and easily understand spiritual realities and can feel strongly touched with "grace."

Body effects of captivated attention. Rapture may be manifest as a wide range of body sensations. "The glory and repose of the soul is so great that the body very perceivably shares in that joy and delight."[16] These experiences can range from intensely pleasurable to intensely painful ones. Sometimes a paradoxical mixture of pleasure and pain fills our awareness. St. Teresa said, "Since the pain is sweet and delightful, we never think we can have enough of this pain."[17]

Rapture seems associated with vital energy, much as sexual energy is. St. John of the Cross wrote of the sensual movements that sometimes occur spontaneously during spiritual practice; he clearly meant what most people would interpret as sexual arousal.[18] With very intense rapture, prolonged waves of orgasmic sensation may flood the body with intense bliss. Skin can become so sensitive that even a faint breeze on the cheek can trigger waves of orgasm. Hindu yogis, who have studied such phenomena for millennia, explain that all vital energy is connected, but that these experiences are definitely not sexual. St. Teresa of Avila reassured her brother about such occurrences: "The soul's joy is so keen that it makes itself felt in the body."[19]

Rapture can also be manifest as intense heaviness, or as being pushed or pulled strongly in one direction. We may feel like we are zooming through space. Involuntary movements may occur at times. St. Teresa was well-acquainted with this: "Some persons say they experience a tightening in the chest and even external bodily movements that they cannot restrain."[20] The force of such movements can literally bounce a person off the meditation seat — or produce levitation. Various energies may be manifest, such as the *kundalini* experience of yoga. It can feel like you are undergoing an exorcism.

Need for guidance.   People prone to intense rapture should be under the guidance of competent helpers who understand such experiences. We must learn not to cling to or encourage such experiences, but also not to push them away, all the while maintaining balanced equanimity. Becoming trapped in greed for such experiences is easy, often very subtle, and impedes further spiritual progress.

St. John of the Cross attributed rapture to the weakness of human nature. He said: "The sensory part of the soul is weak and incapable of vigorous spiritual communications [so] these proficients, because of such communications experienced in the sensitive part, suffer many infirmities, injuries, and weaknesses of stomach, and as a result fatigue of spirit."[21]

FOURTH STAGE OF CONCENTRATION

At the fourth stage of absorption, all rapture phenomena fall away.[22] Meditators may be especially aware of how calm the practice feels. We are left in quite still one-pointed repose and equanimity. Sometimes words completely disappear, and we are left only with attention held captive to the meditation object.

Delicate experience. St. Teresa said: "The soul rejoices incomparably more; but it can show much less since no power remains in the body, nor does the soul have any power to communicate its joy. At such a time, everything would be a great obstacle and a torment and a hindrance to its repose."[23] We may feel a very delicate sense of gentle rising or fullness. "The soul sometimes goes forth from itself. The way this happens is comparable to what happens when a fire is burning and...the flame then shoots very high above the fire."[24] We also feel a strong disinclination to move.

Fading of body experience. While pauses in the breath may have occurred even before the first stage of absorption, here they may become lengthy. "It feels with the most marvelous and gentlest delight that everything is almost fading away through a kind of swoon in which breathing and all the bodily energies gradually fail. This experience comes about in such a way that one cannot even stir the hands without a lot of effort."[25] Often there is a complete loss of awareness of body experience. "The time...the soul remains in this suspension of all the faculties is very short; should it remain suspended for a half hour, this would be a very long time.... It is true that since there is no sensory consciousness one finds it hard to know what is happening."[26]

FIFTH STAGE OF CONCENTRATION

Experience in the fifth stage of concentration is extremely subtle. Even happy delight falls away, and only one-pointedness and pervasive equanimity remain.[27] The first three *brahmavihara* practices (loving-kindness, compassion, and sympathetic joy) can bring us only to the fourth stage; equanimity can reach this one.[28]

Although St. Teresa mentioned only four ways to water the garden, she went on to describe another kind of prayer. "The Lord gathers up the soul...in the way the clouds gather up the earthly vapors and raises it completely out of itself. The cloud ascends to heaven and brings the soul along."[29] Being in a cloud is certainly more saturating than even heavy rainfall!

Deep trance. Body functions such as the breath sometimes cease for long periods of time at this stage. "It seems that the soul is not animating the body. Thus there is a very strong feeling that the natural bodily heat is failing it. The body gradually grows cold, although this happens with the greatest ease and delight. At this stage there is no remedy that can be used to resist."[30] All sense of the body may disappear. When it is present, the body can feel like it has no connection with the meditator, or like a "thing" with which the meditator can do nothing. "Thus, however hard I try to stir, there is not strength enough in the body for a good while to be able to do so; the soul carries off with it all this strength."[31]

Taste of heaven. "From this prayer comes the pain of having to return to everyday life.... The soul sees very clearly how little everything here below should be esteemed and the trifle that it is.... The soul no longer wants to desire."[32] We can truly feel as if we have experienced the highest joy possible and want nothing but it. Earth holds no delights to compare. "How painful it is for a soul who finds itself in this stage to have to return to dealing with everything, to behold and see the farce of this so poorly harmonized life, to waste time in taking care of bodily needs, sleeping, and eating! Everything wearies it; it doesn't know how to flee; it sees itself captured and in chains. Then it feels more truly the misery of life."[33] We now want only God.

POSTSCRIPT

CONTINUING YOUR *METTA* PRACTICE

Now that you understand *brahmavihara* practice — both how to do it and the theoretical background from which it comes — what do you do next? Here are some suggestions.

You can get a good start on your practice from this book, but most people find progress comes more quickly when they do regular retreats or work with a teacher. The support of like-minded people also helps. To find retreats or sitting groups, contact either IMS or RES.[1]

IMS (Insight Meditation Society) offers retreats in a purely Buddhist setting; they regularly schedule *metta* retreats. RES (Resources for Ecumenical Spirituality) offers some retreats in Buddhist framework only and also offers ecumenically oriented retreats — primarily Christian-Buddhist.

THE OTHER THERAVADAN PRACTICE, INSIGHT MEDITATION

I also strongly encourage you to learn the other Theravadan Buddhist practice, insight practice. You may want to read *Purifying the Heart: Buddhist Insight Meditation for Christians,* by Culligan, Meadow, and Chowning; it is also published by Crossroad. If you work well with cassette tapes, Credence Cassettes in Kansas City has published the RES 1991 Silence and Awareness retreat, teaching insight meditation as a method for the spirituality of St. John of the Cross. You can also find retreats in insight practice through both RES and IMS.

YOUR EXAMINATION ON *METTA*

In chapter 5, I promised you an examination after your *metta* training. Here it is, as presented in the *Visuddhimagga*.[2]

You are captured by kidnappers along with a loved bene-factor, a dear friend, someone you do not know well at all (a neutral person), and someone who has done you wrong ("the enemy"). The kidnappers say they are going to kill one person, and you must decide who it is to be. What is your answer?

If you immediately leapt to offering any of the people, you fail the exam. If you started to weigh the pros and cons of the value of each person to you, you fail the exam. If you try to weigh objectively the value of each life to the world as a whole, you fail the exam. If you think you ought to sacrifice yourself for the sake of the others, you fail the exam. The classically correct answer is to be absolutely unable to come to a decision. All the boundaries between yourself and others, and the boundaries between all these others, have been so erased that you are incapable of any discrimination among people. Please do not feel bad if you failed the exam. Many people who practice *metta* do not get to this dispassion easily.

May your spiritual practice continue to grow. May it bring you the fullness of all blessings, and lead you home to God.

SANGHA[3]

Softly chanting *metta*
Into the sun-drenched breeze,
I sit by Stillness Pond.[4]
A dragonfly alighting on my knee
Looks quizzically up at me.
I stop my chant; she leaves.
Again I start, and she returns.

Rest easy, Sister, bide a while.
I will stay and chant to you,
Awake perhaps some memory
Long lain fallow in endless time.
May you reclaim your heritage.
Sabbe vinipatika anigha hontu.[5]

Appendix I

Instructions for Chanting Tones

The chants that appear in the following appendices have been adapted for group chanting in plain chant. The punctuation and underlining of this copy facilitate the singing of these chants in Psalm Tone 8, Gregorian Chant. The particular beauty of Psalm Tone 8 is its simplicity; it is an unassuming servant of sung prayer.

The text is set up in two-line verses. The asterisk at the middle of the verse calls for a slight slowing in the preceding few syllables. The period at the end of the verse calls for slightly more slowing in the preceding syllables. This is not to be exaggerated but should flow naturally, almost unobtrusively, from the rhythm of the sung language.

Each psalm tone is characterized by the dominance of a single tone with a unique melody pattern at the middle and at the end of the verse. The underlining of a syllable indicates the first change in pitch before the asterisk or before the ending. Usually, there is one tone for each syllable at the end of each line. When there is an extra syllable, it is sung on the final tone for the line.

On the following page are the tones to be used for each successive two lines of chant. The tones given are for the middle range of the scale, which both women and men should be able to sound. It is entirely possible to move the range up or down, so long as the same intervals between tones are maintained. One could also set the chant to an entirely different intonation.

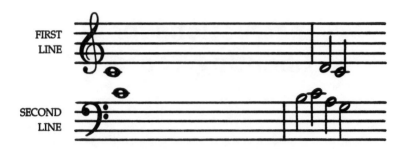

Appendix II

Metta (Loving-Kindness) Chant

(Appendix I gives instructions for chanting in plain chant tones. It explains the underlining and asterisks.)

Preparation with Forgiveness

I ask forgiveness of all <u>be</u>ings*
Whom I have hurt or <u>harmed</u> in any way.
I freely forgive all beings who have <u>harmed</u> me.*
I free<u>ly</u> forgive myself.

Pervasion of Loving-Kindness

May I be safe from inner and outer <u>danger</u>.*
May I be protected from <u>harm</u> and enmity.
May I be happy and free of mental <u>torment</u>.*
May I be peaceful in <u>heart</u> and clear in mind.
May I be free of physical af<u>flic</u>tion.*
May my body be <u>strong</u> and healthy.
May I take care of <u>myself</u> <u>eas</u>ily.*
May I tend my <u>life</u> with gladness.

My mother and my <u>fa</u>ther,*
All my teachers and <u>oth</u>er helpers,
All my friends and all my <u>rela</u>tives,*
And all others who <u>walk</u> the path with me.

Refrain 1

> May they be safe from inner and outer <u>dan</u>ger.*
> May they be protected from <u>harm</u> and enmity.
> May they be happy and free of mental <u>tor</u>ment.*
> May they be peaceful in <u>heart</u> and clear in mind.
> May they be free of physical af<u>flic</u>tion.*
> May their bodies be <u>strong</u> and healthy.
> May they take care <u>of</u> themselves <u>eas</u>ily.*
> May they tend their <u>lives</u> with gladness.

(Verse for monastic and retreat settings)

All those gathered in this <u>sa</u>cred place,*
All those in <u>every</u> walk of life,
All those who are taking <u>care</u> of us,*
And all the heavenly <u>guar</u>dians watching.

Refrain 1

All existent <u>be</u>ings,*
All those <u>who</u> have breath of life,
All distinct creatures, all indi<u>vi</u>duals,*
All embodied <u>per</u>sonalities.

Refrain 1

Refrain 2

> May they be free of all pain, distress, and tribu<u>la</u>tion,*
> May they come to the end <u>of</u> all suffering.
> May what good they have remain with them and grow
>   <u>great</u>er,*
> May <u>they</u> enjoy unending happiness <u>and</u> abundance.
> Yet their joys and sorrows of the <u>fu</u>ture*
> Depend upon their actions and <u>not</u> my wishes.

All beings who are <u>fe</u>male,*
And <u>all</u> male beings.
All those who are <u>saint</u>ly,*
And all those not yet <u>come</u> to holiness.

All angels and all human be<u>ings</u>,*
And all those in <u>states</u> of suffering.

Refrain 1

Refrain 2

In the eastern and western di<u>rec</u>tions,*
In the northern and south<u>ern</u> directions,
To the southeast and to the <u>north</u>west,*
To the northeast and <u>to</u> the southwest.
In the downward di<u>rec</u>tion,*
And in the up<u>ward</u> direction.
All existent be<u>ings</u>,*
All those <u>who</u> have breath of life,
All distinct creatures, all indi<u>vi</u>duals,*
All embodied <u>per</u>sonalities.
All beings who are <u>fe</u>male,*
And <u>all</u> male beings.
All those who are <u>saint</u>ly,*
And all those not yet <u>come</u> to holiness.
All angels and all human be<u>ings</u>,*
And all those in <u>states</u> of suffering.

Refrain 1

Refrain 2

As far up as the highest ex<u>ist</u>ence,*
And as far down <u>as</u> the lowest,
In the entire <u>uni</u>verse,*
Whatever be<u>ings</u> that move on earth,
May they be <u>free</u> from distress and <u>threat</u> of harm,*
From physical suffer<u>ing</u> and danger.

As far up as the highest ex<u>ist</u>ence,*
And as far down <u>as</u> the lowest,
In the entire <u>uni</u>verse,*
Whatever beings that <u>move</u> in water,
May they be free from distress and <u>threat</u> of harm,*

From physical suffering and danger.

As far up as the highest existence,*
And as far down as the lowest,
In the entire universe,*
Whatever beings that move in air,
May they be free from distress and threat of harm,*
From physical suffering and danger.

By the power of all that is holy,*
As shown in the lives of holy people,
I call down protection in every way,*
In each direction.

Closing Offerings

Surely by this practice*
From the wages of sin I shall be freed.
May the merit of this practice*
Destroy the roots of harmful tendencies.
May the merits of this practice*
Lead me to greater knowledge and love of God.
May the merit of this practice*
Be for the good of of all beings.

Amen.*

Amen. Amen.

This chant is our translation of one from a Malaysian Theravadan Buddhist monastery, where it is chanted in the evening. It includes all beings blessed and the traditional blessings used in Theravadan Buddhist loving-kindness, compassion, sympathetic joy, and equanimity practices. These practices are designed to foster universal, non-discriminating good will toward all beings.

Appendix III

Pali Words for the Pervasion of *Metta*

If you prefer to offer *metta* in the Pali language, the phrases are given below. The meaning of the words is explained in chapter 5 of this book.

Sending *metta* to oneself:

Avero (uh-weh-roh) *homi* (hoh'-mee).
Abyapajjho (uhb-yah'-puhj-joh') *homi.*
Anigho (uh-nee'-goh) *homi.*
Sukhi (soo'-kee) *attanam* (uh-tuh'-nuhm) *pariharami* (puh'-ree-huh-rah'-mee)

**Sending *metta* to individuals,
addressing them as "you":**

Avera (uh-weh'-rah) *hotu* (hoh'-too).
Abyapajjha (uhb-yah'-puhj-jah') *hotu.*
Anigha (uh-nee'-gah) *hotu.*
Sukhi (soo'-kee) *attanam* (uh-tuh'-nuhm) *pariharatu* (puh'-ree-huh-ruh'-too).

Sending *metta* to the general universal categories:

Sabbe (suh-bay) *satta* (suh-tah) *avera* (uh-weh'-rah) *hontu* (hohn-too).
Sabbe satta abyapajjha (uhb-yah'-puhj-jah') *hontu.*

Sabbe satta anigha (uh-nee'-gah) *hontu.*
Sabbe satta sukhi (soo'-kee) *attanam* (uh-tuh'-nuhm)
   pariharantu (puh'-ree-huh-ruhn'-too).

Sabbe pana (pah-nah) ...
Sabbe bhuta (bhoo-tah) ...
Sabbe puggala (poo'-guh-lah) ...
Sabbe attabhava (uh-tuh-bhah'-wuh) *pariyapanna* (par'-ee-
   yah-puh'-nah) ...

Sending *metta* to the particular universal categories:

Sabba (suh-bah) *itthiyo* (ee'-tee-yoh) *avera* (uh-weh'-rah)
   hontu (hohn-too).
Sabba itthiyo abyapajjha (uhb-yah'-puhj-jah') *hontu.*
Sabba itthiyo anigha (uh-nee'-gah) *hontu.*
Sabba itthiyo sukhi (soo'-kee) *attanam* (uh-tuh'-nuhm)
   pariharantu (puh'-ree-huh-ruhn'-too).
Sabbe (suh-bay) *purisa* (pooh'-ree-sah) ...

Sabbe ariya (uh'-ree-yah) ...
Sabbe anariya (uhn'-uh-ree-yah) ...
Sabbe deva (deh'-wah) ...
Sabbe manussa (muh-noos'-sah) ...
Sabbe vinipatika (wee'-nee-pah'-tee-kah) ...

Alternative Phrases for *Metta* (Loving-Kindness) and Other *Brahmaviharas* (Compassion, Gladness, and Equanimity)

These phrases are offered for people using traditional phrases who find the ones given either too short or too long for comfortable use. Sometimes a phrase of one length that has worked well starts feeling too long or too short. Below are classical phrases of various lengths from which to choose.

For *Metta* (loving-kindness):

1a. May they be safe from inner and outer danger; may they be protected from harm and enmity.

1b. May they be safe from harm and danger.

1c. May they be safe.

2a. May they be happy and free of mental torment; may they be peaceful in heart and clear in mind.

2b. May they be happy and peaceful in mind.

2c. May they be peaceful (or happy).

3a. May they be free of physical affliction; may their bodies be strong and healthy.

3b. May they be strong and healthy in body.

3c. May they be healthy.

4a. May they take care of themselves easily; may they tend their lives with gladness.

4b. May they tend their lives with happy ease.

4c. May they have ease.

For *Karuna* (compassion)

a. May they be free of pain, distress, and tribulation; may they come to the end of all suffering.

b. May they be free of all pain and suffering.

c. May they be free of suffering.

For *Mudita* (sympathetic joy)

a. May what good they have remain and grow greater; may they enjoy unending happiness and abundance.

b. May their happiness and success never end.

c. May they stay happy.

For *Upekkha* (equanimity)

a. Their joys and sorrows of the future depend upon their actions and not my wishes.

b. Their outcomes depend on their choices, not wishes.

c. They reap what they sow.

Appendix V

Metta (Loving-Kindness) Chant for Human Beings

(See Appendix I for instructions on how to chant in plain chant tones. This explains the underlined words and asterisks.)

All people without any exception,*
All female and all male people,*
All people both strong and feeble,*
All tall people and all all short people,
All people both small and large,*
All I have met and all I have never seen,
All people dwelling both far and near,*
All people already born and those not yet born.

Refrain

May they be safe from inner and outer danger.*
May they be protected from harm and enmity.
May they be happy and free of mental torment.*
May they be peaceful in heart and clear in mind.
May they be free of physical affliction.*
May their bodies be strong and healthy.
May they take care of themselves easily.*
May they tend their lives with gladness.
May they be free of all pain, distress, and tribulation,*
May they come to the end of all suffering.
May what good they have remain with them and grow
    greater,*

May they enjoy unending happiness <u>and</u> abundance.
Yet their joys and sorrows of the <u>future</u>*
Depend upon their actions and <u>not</u> my wishes.

All people living <u>every</u>where,*
All in my community and nation,
All people in the eastern di<u>rection</u>,*
Those in Mediterranean, Slavic, and Se<u>mit</u>ic places,
All people in the western di<u>rection</u>,*
Those in India, southern, and <u>south</u>east Asia,
All people in the northern di<u>rection</u>,*
Those in the lands of Native Americans <u>and</u> the North Pole,
All people in the southern di<u>rection</u>,*
Those in Latin America <u>and</u> Antarctica,

All people in the southeastern di<u>rection</u>,*
Those peo<u>ple</u> in Africa,
All people <u>in</u> the northwestern di<u>rection</u>,*
Those in China, Russia, Japan, and all <u>northern</u> Asia,
All people in the northeastern di<u>rection</u>,*
Those in Anglo, Baltic, Germanic, and <u>Nor</u>dic places,
All people in the southwestern di<u>rection</u>,*
Those in Australia and the <u>South</u> Pacific.

Refrain

All people of every racial and <u>eth</u>nic stock*
Across the whole range of <u>human</u> diversity,
All people of African <u>heri</u>tage,*
All people of East <u>A</u>sian heritage,
All people of European <u>heri</u>tage,*
All people of Latin Ameri<u>can</u> heritage,
All people of Mid-Eastern <u>heri</u>tage,*
All people of Native Ameri<u>can</u> heritage,
All people of South Pacific <u>heri</u>tage,*
All people of mixed <u>ra</u>cial heritage.

Refrain

All people of <u>every</u> age,*

All those <u>wai</u>ting to be born,
All babies and all young <u>chil</u>dren,*
All teenaged children <u>and</u> all young adults,
All mid-aged and all mature-aged <u>a</u>dults,*
All elderly and ve<u>ry</u> old adults.

Refrain

All human <u>be</u>ings,*
All <u>in</u>dividuals,
All members of the <u>hu</u>man race,*
All peo<u>ple</u>, all persons.

Refrain

This chant is adapted for human beings from a Malaysian Theravadan Buddhist chant. The first verse lists beings toward whom the Buddha said blessings should be sent; the directions are from traditional *metta* practice. Refrain of the chant is adapted from the traditional blessings used in Theravadan Buddhist loving-kindness, compassion, sympathetic joy, and equanimity practices. These practices are designed to foster universal, non-discriminating good will toward all beings.

Appendix VI

Metta (Loving-Kindness) Chant for Animals

(See Appendix I for instructions on how to chant in plain chant tones. This explains the underlined words and asterisks.)

All huge animals like elephants and whales,*
All large animals like horses cows, and tigers,
All medium-sized animals like cats, dogs, goats, and
    monkeys,*
All small animals like fish, birds rats, and chipmunks,
All tiny animals like butterflies, worms, and insects,*
All minute animals too small to be seen.

Refrain

    May they be safe from inner and outer danger.*
    May they be protected from harm and enmity.
    May they be happy and free of mental torment.*
    May they be peaceful in heart and clear in mind.
    May they be free of physical affliction.*
    May their bodies be strong and healthy.
    May they take care of themselves easily.*
    May they tend their lives with gladness.
    May they be free of all pain, distress, and tribulation,*
    May they come to the end of all suffering.
    May what good they have remain with them and grow
        greater,*
    May they enjoy unending happiness and abundance.

Yet their joys and sorrows of the future*
Depend upon their actions and not my wishes.

All animals that move underground,*
All animals that move on land,
All animals that move in water,*
All animals that move in air.

Refrain

All simple spineless animals like jellyfish and sponges,*
All worms, snails, leeches, clams, and like animals,
All insects and all spiders,*
All fish like carp, cod, trout, and salmon,
All amphibians like frogs, toads, and salamanders,*
All reptiles like lizards, turtles, snakes, and crocodiles,
All birds like gulls, ducks, finch, bluejays, and robins,*
All mammals like baboons, sheep, pigs, and antelope.

Refrain

All animals that live in bogs and marshes,*
All animals that live in cities,
All animals that live in deserts,*
All animals that live on farmland,
All animals that live in woods and forests,*
All animals that live on glaciers and ice packs,
All animals that live on heath and tundra,*
All animals that live in jungles,
All animals that live in lakes and ponds,*
All animals that live in meadows,
All animals that live on mountains,*
All animals that live in seas and oceans,
All animals that live on plains,*
All animals that live in streams and rivers,
All animals that live in vales and valleys,*
All animals living anywhere.

Refrain

The refrain of this chant is adapted from the traditional blessings used in Theravadan Buddhist loving-kindness, compassion, sympathetic joy, and equanimity practices. These practices are designed to foster universal, non-discriminating good will toward all beings.

Appendix VII

Loving-Kindness Chant for Other Realms of Existence

(See Appendix I for instructions on how to chant in plain chant tones. This explains the underlined words and asterisks.)

All seraphim and all cherubim*
Who exist only to sing praise to God,
All thrones who bring justice,*
All powers who protect people from evil,
All dominions who regulate life in heaven,*
All virtues who work miracles,
All principalities protecting nations,*
All archangels and all angels who care for people.

Refrain

May they be safe from inner and outer danger.*
May they be protected from harm and enmity.
May they be happy and free of mental torment.*
May they be peaceful in heart and clear in mind.
May they be free of physical affliction.*
May their bodies be strong and healthy.
May they take care of themselves easily.*
May they tend their lives with gladness.
May they be free of all pain, distress, and tribulation,*
May they come to the end of all suffering.
May what good they have remain with them and grow
  greater,*

May they enjoy unending happiness <u>and</u> abundance.
Yet their joys and sorrows of the <u>future</u>*
Depend upon their actions and <u>not</u> my wishes.

All brahma beings with utterly <u>pure</u> minds,*
Engrossed in the bliss of free<u>dom</u> from torment,
All bright, shining deva <u>beings</u>*
Crowned with virtue and generosity,
All helpful beings in the <u>higher</u> realms,*
All beings of hea<u>ven</u>ly character.

Refrain

All <u>hungry</u> ghosts*
Who never <u>can</u> be satisfied,
All those captured in de<u>mon</u>ic minds,*
All unquiet spirits <u>who</u> may roam the earth,
All those in various states of <u>suffering</u>,*
All consumed by un<u>whole</u>some mind states.

Refrain

All beings in various <u>hell</u> realms,*
All carnal ones aban<u>doned</u> to passions,
All gluttons wallowing in <u>pleasures</u>,*
All hoarders and wasters <u>loving</u> money,
All beings who are wrathful and <u>sullen</u>,*
All those who refuse to ac<u>knowledge</u> the truth,
All those who engage in violence of <u>any</u> kind,*
Who attack others, them<u>selves</u>, or the truth,
All fraudulent ones taking advantage of <u>others</u>,*
All malicious ones acting in treachery,
All whose minds embrace any kind of <u>ill</u> will,*
All in the darkness <u>of</u> consuming hate.

Refrain

All beings in various states of <u>purgation</u>,*
All those <u>not</u> yet pure of heart,
All who suffer results of past bad <u>conduct</u>,*

All who are being cleansed of men<u>tal</u> impurity.

Refrain

All beings in the highest <u>purest</u> realms,*
All beings in realms <u>of</u> good character,
All beings in places of <u>suffering</u>,*
All non-human <u>beings</u> everywhere.

Refrain

The refrain of this chant is adapted from the traditional blessings used in Theravadan Buddhist loving-kindness, compassion, sympathetic joy, and equanimity practices. These practices are designed to foster universal, non-discriminating good will toward all beings.

Notes

Preface

1. St. Teresa of Avila, *The Collected Works of St. Teresa of Avila,* trans. Kieran Kavanaugh and Otilio Rodriguez (Washington D.C.: Institute of Carmelite Studies, 1976); St. John of the Cross, *The Collected Works of St. John of the Cross,* rev. ed., trans. Kieran Kavanaugh and Otilio Rodriguez (Washington D.C.: Institute of Carmelite Studies, 1991).

2. Buddhaghosa, *Visuddhimagga (The Path of Purification): The Classic Manual of Buddhist Doctrine and Meditation,* 4th ed., trans. Bhikkhu Nyanamoli (Kandy, Sri Lanka: Buddhist Publication Society, 1979); Mahasi Sayadaw, *Brahmavihara Dhamma* (Rangoon, Burma: Buddha Sasana Nuggaha Organization, 1985).

3. Forthcoming from Crossroad Publishing Co.

4. *Nostra Aetate* (Declaration on the Relationship of the Church to Non-Christian Religions), no. 2; and *Ad Gentes* (Decree on the Church's Missionary Activity), no. 18.

5. Insight Meditation Society, 1230 Pleasant Street, Barre, MA 01005. You can get on their mailing list by request.

6. For information about RES retreats or other projects, write to RES, P.O. Box 6, Mankato, MN 56002, or RES, Route 1, Box 1160, Dunnegan, MO 65640.

Chapter 1: To Love without Fear

1. For a slightly different translation and a discussion of this, see Mahasi Sayadaw, *Brahmavihara Dhamma* (Rangoon, Burma: Buddha Sasana Nuggaha Organization, 1985), 79.

2. *Metta Sutta,* from the *Sutta Nipata:* 143–52.

3. *Dhammapada,* no. 5. (*Majjhima Nikaya, Sutta* 128).

4. *Sutta* 27, from the *Itivuttaka.*

5. *Nidana Vagga,* from the *Samyutta Nikaya,* 20:3.

6. The reasons for this are explained in chapter 9. The appropriate people to whom to send *metta* are described in Buddhaghosa, *Visuddhimagga (The Path of Purification): The Classic Manual of Buddhist Doctrine and Meditation,* 4th ed., trans. Bhikkhu Nyanamoli (Kandy, Sri Lanka: Buddhist Publication Society, 1979), 9:4–7.

7. *Metta Sutta.*

8. *Patisambhidamagga.*

9. We discuss compassion, sympathetic joy, and equanimity, the other heavenly states of mind, in more detail in chapter 7.

10. *Dhammapada,* no. 5.

Chapter 2: Burning Up Your Support

1. Buddhaghosa, *Visuddhimagga (The Path of Purification): The Classic Manual of Buddhist Doctrine and Meditation,* 4th ed., trans. Bhikkhu Nyanamoli (Kandy, Sri Lanka: Buddhist Publication Society, 1979), 9:98.

2. Ibid., 9:1–3.

3. See Mahasi Sayadaw, *Brahmavihara Dhamma* (Rangoon, Burma: Buddha Sasana Nuggaha Organization, 1985), 5–6.

4. *Samyutta Nikaya,* 46:55.

5. *Anguttara Nikaya, Sattaka-nipata:* 60.

6. *Anguttara Nikaya,* 1:216.

7. *Anguttara Nikaya,* Book of Threes: 53.

8. Ibid., 68.

9. *Dhammapada,* nos. 3–4.

10. *Anguttara Nikaya, Pancaka-nipata* (Book of Fives): 161.

11. *Samyutta Nikaya,* 7:1, 2.

12. P. A. Sorokin, "The Powers of Creative Unselfish Love," in A. H. Maslow, ed., *New Knowledge in Human Values* (Chicago: Regnery, 1971), 3–12.

13. *Visuddhimagga,* 9:14–39.

14. *Samyutta Nikaya,* 1:162.

Chapter 3: Toward Heart-Deliverance

1. Buddhaghosa, *Visuddhimagga (The Path of Purification): The Classic Manual of Buddhist Doctrine and Meditation*, 4th ed., trans. Bhikkhu Nyanamoli (Kandy, Sri Lanka: Buddhist Publication Society, 1979), 1:18.
2. *Anguttara Nikaya*, Book of Fours: 165.
3. *Sutta-Nipata, Mahamangala Sutta*: 265–66.
4. *Samyutta Nikaya* 1:222.
5. Sayadaw U Pandita, *In This Very Life: The Liberation Teachings of the Buddha* (Boston: Wisdom Publications, 1992), 52. U Pandita is a chief disciple of Mahasi Sayadaw.
6. St. Teresa of Avila, *Life*, 15:6, in *The Collected Works of St. Teresa of Avila*, trans. Kieran Kavanaugh and Otilio Rodriguez (Washington D.C.: Institute of Carmelite Studies, 1976).
7. *Dhammapada*, no. 184.
8. *Majjhima Nikaya (Kakucapamasutta)*, 1:124.
9. Ibid., 128–29.
10. *Samyutta Nikaya*, 8:1–2.
11. *Jataka*, 3:39.
12. *Ekadasa Nipata 16*, from *Anguttara Nikaya*.
13. *Visuddhimagga*, 9:61.
14. *Devas* are discussed in more detail in chapter 9.
15. The *Visuddhimagga* refers to several of these stories in chapter 9:71–72.

Chapter 4: Rejoicing Hearts

1. *Metta Sutta*, from the *Sutta Nipata*, verses 143–52.
2. See Mahasi Sayadaw, *Brahmavihara Dhamma* (Rangoon, Burma: Buddha Sasana Nuggaha Organization, 1985), 85–111.
3. Ibid., 107.
4. Ibid., 13.
5. *Digha Nikaya (Sigalavadasutta)*, 3:186–87.
6. Ibid.
7. *Samyutta Nikaya*, 45:2.
8. Ibid., 3:1, 4.
9. *Dhammapada*, nos. 76–77.

Chapter 5: Getting Ready to Love

1. I am indebted to Andrew Olendzki of Insight Meditation Society for help with Pali phrases. The full phrases in Pali, with phonetic pronunciation, are in Appendix III.

2. Sharon Salzberg, co-founder of and a guiding teacher at Insight Meditation Society. Her book on *metta* is in press and will be published by Shambhala.

3. See Mahasi Sayadaw, *Brahmavihara Dhamma* (Rangoon, Burma: Buddha Sasana Nuggaha Organization, 1985), 15–16.

4. *Nidana Samyutta, Okkha Sutta.*

5. *Samyutta Nikaya* 3:1, 8 *(Mallika).*

6. Buddhaghosa, *Visuddhimagga (The Path of Purification): The Classic Manual of Buddhist Doctrine and Meditation*, 4th ed., trans. Bhikkhu Nyanamoli (Kandy, Sri Lanka: Buddhist Publication Society, 1979), 9:4–7.

7. Ibid., 9:5.

8. Ibid., 9:41.

Chapter 6: Filling the World with Love

1. *Samyutta Nikaya* I:75; *Udana* 47.

Chapter 7: Abodes of the Gods

1. See Mahasi Sayadaw, *Brahmavihara Dhamma* (Rangoon, Burma: Buddha Sasana Nuggaha Organization, 1985), 1.

2. Insight, or *vipassana* practice, is the other major practice of Theravadan Buddhism. For information on insight practice, see Culligan, Meadow, and Chowning, *Purifying the Heart: Buddhist Insight Practice for Christians* (New York: Crossroad, forthcoming). Or write to RES, P.O. Box 6, Mankato, MN 56001, or RES, Route 1, Box 1160, Dunnegan, MO 65640.

3. Matrceta, "Hymn to the Buddha of Infinite Compassion and Wisdom," from the *Satapancasatka.*

4. Buddhaghosa, *Visuddhimagga (The Path of Purification): The Classic Manual of Buddhist Doctrine and Meditation*, 4th ed., trans. Bhikkhu Nyanamoli (Kandy, Sri Lanka: Buddhist Publication Society, 1979), 9:92.

5. Chapter 9 discusses rebirth and other realms of existence.

Chapter 8: Overcoming Hatred with Love

1. *Dhammapada,* no. 182.

Chapter 9: Blessing All Beings

1. Buddhaghosa, *Visuddhimagga (The Path of Purification): The Classic Manual of Buddhist Doctrine and Meditation,* 4th ed., trans. Bhikkhu Nyanamoli (Kandy, Sri Lanka: Buddhist Publication Society, 1979), 1:17.

2. I am not suggesting that Jesus "became" a *deva.* However, qualities of his risen body — such as being able to go through solid objects and yet still eat and embrace people — are common characteristics ascribed to *devas.* Similarly, as was the case with Jesus, *devas* look much like human beings when they manifest themselves; however, there are still some things different, such as those that made the disciples' identification of the risen Jesus feel uncertain at first.

3. F. X. Schouppe, *Purgatory: Explained by the Lives and Legends of the Saints* (Rockford Ill.: Tan Books, 1986).

4. Kenneth Woodward, et al., "Angels," in *Newsweek,* December 27, 1993.

5. Nancy Gibbs, "Angels among Us," in *Time,* December 27, 1993.

6. *The Celestial Hierarchy,* in *Pseudo-Dionysius: The Complete Works,* trans. Colm Luibheid (New York: Paulist Press, 1987).

7. Dante, "Inferno," in *Divine Comedy.* Available in many editions.

Chapter 10: Ways to Taste Heaven

1. Chapter 12 discusses different levels of concentration.

2. Buddhaghosa, *Visuddhimagga (The Path of Purification): The Classic Manual of Buddhist Doctrine and Meditation,* 4th ed., trans. Bhikkhu Nyanamoli (Kandy, Sri Lanka: Buddhist Publication Society, 1979), 3:3.

3. For more information on insight practice, see Culligan, Meadow, and Chowning, *Purifying the Heart: Buddhist Insight Practice for Christians* (New York: Crossroad, forthcoming). Or write to RES, P.O. Box 6, Mankato, MN 56001, or RES, Route 1, Box 1160, Dunnegan, MO 65640. The *Visuddhimagga* (above) discusses it in great detail in part 3, chapters 14–23.

4. The different levels of concentration are explained more completely in chapter 12.

5. *Devas* and *nibbana* were discussed in chapter 9. The Ten Recollections are discussed in the *Visuddhimagga*, chapters 7 and 8.

6. *Visuddhimagga*, 9:118.

7. For one example in medicine, see Herbert Benson, *The Relaxation Response* (New York: William Morrow, 1975); also available in Bantam paper edition. For psychology many studies are cited in *The Psychology of Meditation*, ed. Michael A. West (New York: Oxford University Press, 1990).

Chapter 11: Not to Be Intimidated!

1. St. Teresa of Avila, *Life*, 13:7, in *The Collected Works of St. Teresa of Avila*, trans. Kieran Kavanaugh and Otilio Rodriguez (Washington D.C.: Institute of Carmelite Studies, 1976).

2. Ibid., 12:5.

3. St. Teresa of Avila, *The Interior Castle*, Fourth Mansions, 3:11, in *Collected Works*.

4. Buddhaghosa, *Visuddhimagga (The Path of Purification): The Classic Manual of Buddhist Doctrine and Meditation*, 4th ed., trans. Bhikkhu Nyanamoli (Kandy, Sri Lanka: Buddhist Publication Society, 1979), 4:86–87, 104.

5. St. John of the Cross, *Spiritual Canticle* 20, 21:9, in *The Collected Works of St. John of the Cross*, rev. ed., trans. Kieran Kavanaugh and Otilio Rodriguez (Washington D.C.: Institute of Carmelite Studies, 1991).

6. St. Teresa of Avila, *Life*, 11:15.

7. Ibid., 11:10.

8. Ibid., 11:13.

9. This classic little work, by an unknown medieval author, is available in different translations and editions. Many consider that by William Johnston to be the best.

10. St. Teresa of Avila, *Life,* 22:9.

11. St. John of the Cross, *Dark Night of the Soul,* Book II, 11:5–6, in *Collected Works.*

Chapter 12: Watering the Garden

1. St. Teresa of Avila, *Life,* 11:7, in *The Collected Works of St. Teresa of Avila,* trans. Kieran Kavanaugh and Otilio Rodriguez (Washington D.C.: Institute of Carmelite Studies, 1976).

2. Buddhaghosa, *Visuddhimagga (The Path of Purification): The Classic Manual of Buddhist Doctrine and Meditation,* 4th ed., trans. Bhikkhu Nyanamoli (Kandy, Sri Lanka: Buddhist Publication Society, 1979), 4:74.

3. St. Teresa of Avila, *Life,* 20:4.

4. *Visuddhimagga,* 4:88–108. These are also discussed in Sayadaw U Pandita, *In This Very Life: The Liberation Teachings of the Buddha* (Boston: Wisdom Publications, 1992), 187–90.

5. St. Teresa of Avila, *Life,* 11:13.

6. Ibid., 11:10.

7. *Visuddhimagga,* 4:139, 199, 202.

8. St. Teresa of Avila, *Life,* 14:4.

9. Ibid., 15:8.

10. St. Teresa of Avila, *The Interior Castle,* Prologue 1; IV, 1:10, in *Collected Works.*

11. For example, see St. John of the Cross, *Ascent of Mount Carmel,* Book II, 19:1 and 19:10, in *The Collected Works of St. John of the Cross,* rev. ed., trans. Kieran Kavanaugh and Otilio Rodriguez (Washington D.C.: Institute of Carmelite Studies, 1991).

12. *Visuddhimagga,* 4:139, 201–2.

13. St. Teresa of Avila, *Life,* 16:3.

14. Ibid., 16:1.

15. Ibid., 17:1.

16. Ibid., 17:8.

17. St. Teresa of Avila, *The Way of Perfection,* 19:9, in *Collected Works.*

18. St. John of the Cross, *Dark Night of the Soul,* Book I, 4:1, in *Collected Works.*

19. St. Teresa of Avila, Letter 163, in *The Letters of St. Teresa of Jesus,* vol. 1, trans. E. Allison Peers (London: Sheed & Ward, 1951), 408.

20. St. Teresa of Avila, *The Interior Castle,* IV, 2:1.

21. St. John of the Cross, *Dark Night of the Soul,* Book II, 1:2.

22. *Visuddhimagga,* 4:153, 202.

23. St. Teresa of Avila, *Life,* 18:1.

24. Ibid., 18:2.

25. Ibid., 18:10.

26. Ibid., 18:2.

27. *Visuddhimagga,* 4:183, 202.

28. Ibid., 9:118.

29. St. Teresa of Avila, *Life,* 20:2.

30. Ibid., 20:3.

31. Ibid., 20:21.

32. Ibid., 20:22.

33. Ibid., 21:6.

Postscript

1. Insight Meditation Society, 1230 Pleasant Street, Barre, MA 01005; Resources for Ecumenical Spirituality, P.O. Box 6, Mankato, MN 56002, or Route 1, Box 1160, Dunnegan, MO 65640.

2. Buddhaghosa, *Visuddhimagga (The Path of Purification): The Classic Manual of Buddhist Doctrine and Meditation,* 4th ed., trans. Bhikkhu Nyanamoli (Kandy, Sri Lanka: Buddhist Publication Society, 1979), 9:41.

3. The *sangha* is the spiritual community.

4. Stillness Pond is at Insight Meditation Society, Barre, Massachusetts.

5. "May all suffering beings be free of fear and trembling."